C000078235

comparonomics

why life is better than you
think, and how to make it
even better

grant j ryan

Copyright © 2022 Grant J Ryan

Grant J Ryan asserts his moral right to be identified as the author of this work.

All rights reserved. No part of this publication may be produced or transmitted in any form or by any means, electronic or mechanical, including photocopying, recording or information storage and retrieval systems, without permission in writing from the copyright holder.

Published by Big Idea Publishing Company

Contact: www.bigideapublishingcompany.com

Website: www.comparonomics.com

A catalogue record for this book is available from the National Library of New Zealand.

ISBN 978-0-473-59466-4 (paperback)

ISBN 978-0-473-59467-1 (EPUB)

Credits: Cover design and emoji – jeroentenberge.com

CONTENTS

Part II
HOW DO WE THINK WE ARE
DOING?

WHAT IS THE PROBLEM?

This book has been brewing for a long time. It started with a nagging sense of inadequacy from economic growth theory studied academically many years ago. It was followed by decades in the real world of technology, business, non-profits and even government (calling government real world is a stretch, I know). The odd thing is that all of us use goods and services that a billionaire couldn't have used 10–15 years ago but there is a widespread belief that wages have been stagnant for years and we were better off in the past.

Before you run screaming at the thought of economic growth theory, consider that economic growth is probably the most universally agreed aim in the history of humanity. It is hard to think of anything else most of the world's leaders agree on. Many of us spend vast quantities of our life being a cog in the economic growth machine. Economic growth determines a lot of what you do every day. It also affects how you think about and interact with people around you. It's worth a little time making sure you understand precisely what economic growth is all about.

This book has nothing to say about the best way to achieve growth. It is an investigation of what economic growth is, whether it measures things adequately, and how it affects our day-to-day behaviour. The explanations and tools in this book are maths free and easy for a layperson to follow. The results, however, are somewhat different from what you might expect. The insights discovered are different from what I expected at the start of this investigation. It changed what I wanted to do and how I think about others. Maybe it will for you too. It is worth considering:

- How much does the pursuit of economic growth affect your day-to-day life?
- How much do you know about what economic growth is?

The mantra of economic growth is so universally accepted across all societies and cultures that any improvement in understanding it has vast ramifications. Tim Harford, author of *The Undercover Economist*, eloquently explains the importance of economics:

> ... this remains a wonderful time to be thinking about economics. It's true that it often seems to let us down, but that is the nature of the challenge: there are few systems that we can study that are as complex and multifaceted as the astonishing economy that has been the cause and consequence of human civilization.

A few observations in the last few years accelerated the development of this book. One was dropping off some rubbish at the local refuse centre and seeing the types of things people left. Many of the items, in full working order, were not on the market 10–15 years ago and if they were, then you had to be wealthy to afford them.

Another observation was seeing a picture of people camping out and queuing for the iPhone 3G in an old magazine. This was a device of intense desirability and pure excitement that five years later you couldn't give away. It seems astonishing how quickly things go from wildly desirable for the rich only to completely free.

I was surprised when reading an old economics book from Joseph Schumpeter talking about how in the 1940s we lived like kings, and if we continued to grow at 2%, all problems would be solved.[1] This is a similar set of thoughts to Keynes who envisioned a future life of leisure.[2] We seem to have all sorts of things and services people in the past could only dream of, yet it appears we are not much happier with how life is progressing. If we believe the core messages in the media, we might think the world is full of doom and gloom.

The first question investigated is 'Are we better off now than in the past?' Rather than answering this by debating detailed historical data, we use a new tool that allows anyone to explain this for themselves. You can decide what is important to you and communicate these views explicitly. It is not about me telling you how things are but giving you a tool, so you can answer and understand for yourself.

Agreeing how things have changed is easier than the vastly harder questions of why things have changed or how they are likely to change in the future. Most books looking at economic trends focus on why things have changed or how they are likely to change in the future given different policies. I leave these harder questions to folks smarter than me and just seek clarification on how things have changed because understanding and agreeing on this is key to understanding how we are progressing.

The new tool developed makes it clear how much better off we are than the past but leads to the more puzzling question, 'Why don't we feel better?' Getting to the nub of this question is essential if we are to work out what changes may be needed to make life feel more fulfilling.

I know the word 'economics' puts a lot of people off, but what is discussed here is economics in the broader sense of the word that is nicely summed up by Niall Kishtainy:[3]

> The word 'economics' might sound a bit dry, and make you think of a load of boring statistics. But all it's really about is how to help people to survive and to be healthy and educated. It's about how people get what they need to live full, happy lives — and why some people don't. If we can solve basic economic questions, maybe we can help everyone to live better lives.

I wrote this book as more of an intellectual mystery where the conclusions are not apparent from the start. The two reasons for this are that it reflects the genuine surprise of what I have found writing this book. More importantly, the new tools can investigate all sorts of alternative problems. If I leave the options open as long as possible, then other creative, intelligent folks will be able to draw some different conclusions that have as much chance of being insightful and useful.

The usual way economics books designed for the general population evolve is that obscure academic papers become influential and are built upon if they are any good. The old orthodoxies start to become replaced by new theories. An author takes the time to simplify all the academic papers to something readable by the general population. My favourite examples of this are *Thinking, Fast and Slow* by Daniel Kahneman[4] and *Nudge* by Richard Thaler and Cass Sunstein.[5] Unfortunately, this process takes decades. I have purposely short-circuited this process for two reasons. The new theory is simple enough for anyone to understand and it shows some different, exciting and, I think, significant results. The main risk for you is that this new way of looking at things may be complete rubbish. This theory has not gone through the decade's process of academic scrutiny. However, it only takes about 10 minutes to read the next chapter, and you will see a tool that is easy to understand and shows an alternative view of economic/social development. I'd back anyone to be able to read and get the gist of this new simple tool and make your mind up about how useful it is.

The book has three parts:

- *Part One: How are we doing?* — a new tool allows you to understand how good life is compared to any time in the past.

- *Part Two: How do we think we are doing?* — the way we think about things can be at odds with reality, and here I dig into a list of information, thinking and social biases that tend to make us think things are not as good as they actually are.
- *Part Three: How can we do better?* — some common things we try to do to make life better are investigated to show why they may not help much. I also suggest a couple of novel alternative solutions that have some promise.

METHOD OF ANALYSIS

This book is purposefully devoid of economic jargon as much as possible. For the examples in this book, you do not need to learn all sorts of terminology, theories, and data although a new infographic tool has been created to allow you to represent the results of your thought experiments.

As an example, to work out if life, and the economy, is getting better, I do not explain Total Factor Productivity or Consumer Price Indices and delve into years of data and trends. I ask what is important in your life and how does what we have now compare to any period in the past. You can make up your mind with a series of mini thought experiments to decide if things are getting better or worse. This style obviously has its pitfalls in that topics of vast size are dealt with in a paragraph or sentence. The jargon and detail of conventional economic analysis are considered by some to be so overwhelming that they are owned by 'a priesthood of experts.'[6] The tools developed here allow anyone to participate for themselves, or they can be used to enable more meaningful engagement with others.

The tools developed can be used for investigating not just economic but other social trends as well. As an example of the analysis style, there are only a couple of paragraphs on the evidence that society is vastly less violent than ever before in history. Luckily for us, bright folks have compiled immensely compelling evidence that documents this progress.[7] While some of the best examples of evidence are referenced, the inevitable nuanced arguments around each topic are not discussed. The preferred method of explanation is to offer a set of cases that are quite often in the extreme. This is typically more powerful and memorable than reams of data. I am purposefully leveraging something called the availability heuristic,[8] which is an academic term for the idea that we tend to remember recent stories more than anything else. For example, rather than list all the data and detailed ways that society is less sexist than in 1970, a few facts are given that seem quite astonishing. In Switzerland some women didn't have the vote, in the US women could not get a credit card without their husband's consent, and it was perfectly legal to rape your wife as much as you liked ... gulp! While we have a long way to go with improving sexism, clearly, we have made progress since then.

I am also purposefully unbalanced with some of our examples. As discussed later there are a series of biases that make us feel pessimistic about progress, so I am countering this gloomy view already out there with in-your-face stories of why things are better (though not always). The analysis tool developed is not inherently optimistic, so you can make up your mind as you go through.

Most new economic theories are presented in great detail but typically in a tiny part of the overall picture. What is presented in this book is a broad sketch of a much larger view. A valid criticism of this work will include the fact that there is no depth in the analysis typical of 'proper' theories. The theories developed here are purposely a sketch, not a detailed painting, for three reasons. First is to keep it manageable size-wise. Second is that the broad outline is compelling and easy for a broad range of people to participate and comprehend. The last reason is that there are more talented painters out there that will do a better job of building out the academically rigorous details. Think of it as a division of labour to allow the painters to fill in the finer points from this sketch. Appendix 1 outlines how to mathematicise the theory along with some pointers to parts that could be fleshed out.

Current economic tools are like a powerful, sophisticated electron microscope that is wonderful for seeing detail but can only be used and understood by specialists. What is created here is a cheap pair of binoculars. The goal of this book is to show you how to use them and scan the horizon. It's surprising and dramatic the different picture it shows compared to what the electron microscope operators tell us. Given the new view on things, there are some thought-provoking insights that pop out.

The other style feature used in this book is that I try to state things in an open questioning way rather than a strong, assertive way. Statements are more likely to be in the form 'this suggests that ...' and 'it could well be that ...' rather than the more assertive 'the data confirms that ...' or 'one can be sure that ...'.

I'm from the school of thought suggested by Dan Gardner in *Future Babble*[9] that the more assertive and confident people are about complicated things, the more likely they are to be wrong. While this referenced people's ability to predict the future, I think it is equally applicable to understanding any complex social issues. This stuff is complicated and unknowable with certainty. Some new tools that give a different perspective have been created. Because it is not presented as assertively as is common doesn't necessarily mean it's not as useful.

TIME PERIODS FOR COMPARISON

The two time periods chosen for analysis are entirely arbitrary and you can complete the thought experiments described by selecting any other time periods of interest to you.

I have chosen to analyse King Louis XVI of France who died at the end of the 18th century. He was selected because his life was so utterly privileged that the peasants revolted and chopped off his head. The first time I saw the Louvre I could see why the starving peasants might have been a bit displeased. The first question to answer is how does our modern life compare to one of the most materially prosperous and privileged kings in history?

The easy question is how much wealthier in real dollars was King Louis XVI than us? Quite a lot, is the short answer — but what does that mean? The relatively straightforward question of 'How much richer was he than us?' is substituted with the more subjective questions, 'How did his life compare to ours when you consider the things that are important to us? Do we live better or worse than King Louis XVI?'

The second period and comparison chosen is a middle-income person in a developed country about 50 years ago in the early 1970s. This is viewed as a golden age by some folks and it is also the period where influential economists think economic growth flattened off.[10] Economists tell us that a significant number of us are no better off than 50 years ago, so it seems like a reasonable period to choose. It sometimes seems the common story is that most of the wealth created in this period has gone to the top 1%, with the average and lower wage folks not changed much. What does it mean to say our income has not risen much for 50 years? Does that mean we are no better off at all?

The new comparonomic graph tool developed shows how anyone can visually represent how they think the world has changed. The reason I spend a reasonable amount of time discussing this is that we need to agree on this, so we can dig into the real reasons why we feel things are not getting better. If we think things are getting worse, an obvious solution is to try to make things better. If things are better, we need to dig into some other reasons why we don't feel so good about progress. This enables us to get to the core of how we might understand what things are and aren't worth doing.

Numerous books highlight how much better the world is and probably more highlight how lousy life is. Most of the other books on progress intertwine with a reason for why the world is changing or how it is going to change in the future. For example, techno-optimistic books like *Abundance*[11] and *The Singularity*[12] show the world is getting better due to technology. Other books explain the cause of progress based on the power of markets or social liberalism.[13] Yet others describe the change as a direct result of the Enlightenment[14] or a combination of reasons. Probably the best book for just stating the case for change and investigating why we think so differently is the book *Factfulness*.[15]

The goal of this book is not to offer any explanation for why things have changed or even if they will continue to change in any particular way. I ask the simple questions 'Have they changed?' and 'By how much?' The view of Nicholas Taleb on the impossibility of understanding history resonates with me:

> History is opaque. You see what comes out, not the script that produces events, the generator of history. There is a fundamental incompleteness in your grasp of such events, since you do not see what's inside the box, how the mechanisms work.[16]

Similarly there are vast quantities of literature on the impossibility of predicting the future. So it is a very purposeful strategy to avoid any explanation of why things have changed or any projections about the future.

I suspect that if you are like most people, myself included, you will struggle not to think about the why and what's next because they are fascinating questions. Arguing for one or the other explanation of progress or future prediction is typically a lot more controversial and is a complication we don't need at this stage.[17]

Historians typically try to work out why things change. Futurists may try to predict what will happen going forward. I am taking an economist/psychologist view of trying to work out what has changed and why we might think that, with the view to coming up with ideas that may make life better.

WHO ARE 'WE'? THE 'MIDDLE BILLION'

In this book, you will see the reference to how do 'we' compare to a time in the past. Assume the 'we' refers to the average person in relatively rich democratic countries. The reason for this definition is that I am delving into the question of why do ordinary people in rich countries seem to feel so gloomy about progress? The tools developed in this book may be used to investigate trends for the whole world or any other part of it.[18] It's not that I don't care about the rest of the world, but the particular problem I am investigating is about this subset of comparatively wealthy people.

There are about 1.2 billion people in the relatively affluent democratic world defined by the OECD.[19] For simplicity, I will ignore the wealthiest 10% and the poorest 10% in each country. It's not that I don't care about what is happening to the wealthy and poor but I am keen to simplify things and think about the overall trends for the bulk in the middle of the bell curve.[20] There are vast differences between the top and bottom of even this group, but let's ignore this too. For now, the 'we' refers to about a billion or so broadly average folks in rich countries — the middle billion.

Most of the middle billion are in Europe, North America, Japan, Australia, and Korea along with a few others. They are a culturally diverse bunch that have all changed at different rates on social and economic trends. I will be making some sweeping generalisations about the middle billion, and it is possible to point to countries in this group where things may not be right. I am trying to forget about the outliers and gauge general trends for most of the middle billion.

Why only the middle billion? The comparonomic tool developed can be used for lots of types of questions, but the plight of the middle billion is so compelling because the reality of how they are doing seems so different from what mainstream models and media tell us.

My background is mainly based in Western countries, so the examples tend to be mostly from the US and Europe, but I have tried to include examples from other countries as well. I want to be explicit about any inherent biases that come from this Western background.

Having set the scene, let's delve into a new tool that makes previously difficult economic comparisons easy and compelling.

PART I
HOW ARE WE DOING?

1
COMPARONOMIC GRAPHS: HOW TO REPRESENT CHANGE OVER TIME

IN THIS CHAPTER, I will explain a simple tool for visually representing how things change over time. For each comparison between two periods, you can choose the following subjective descriptions:

- Unbelievably better
- Much better
- Pretty much the same
- Much worse
- Horrifically worse.

Comparing our lives to King Louis XVI has been chosen as it is a simple, non-controversial way to demonstrate the tool. If we use standard economics to compare King Louis's income to ours, then he was vastly more affluent than us. Most of our families cannot afford to employ 36,000 people to build our summer palace or have a couple of thousand maintain it. By some estimates, he was worth about two billion dollars in today's money, but the details don't matter so much. We can assume he was vastly wealthier than us, but what does that mean?

The first comparisons are selected because they are easy to demonstrate how things change. For example, with housing, some things may be better like sanitation, lighting, heating, and cooling, but some things are worse like size and bling. To demonstrate the new tool, I choose to compare the size of housing. With transport, I compare the speed of transportation. This allows us to demonstrate how to build up a picture without having to debate the details. We can then plot these views on a simple graph to build up a picture of how time periods compare. In the examples below, your opinions of how I have made the comparisons could be different. That doesn't matter as the point is to demonstrate a tool for building up a picture of how you think things compare over different time periods. In the next chapter, I will show how you could use more objective data to build a view that may reflect the economy overall but, for now, let's start making some plots to explain how it works.

Take a simple example of the size of one's home. Clearly, King Louis XVI had a much larger home than the average person these days (his summer palace at Versailles was okay too). The comparonomic graph below shows this comparison.

When comparing the past with now, start with the question, 'Would you swap what you have now for then?' That gives the direction of the line. How strongly you think about that will provide the slope of the line.

HOW TO SHOW DIRECTION AND SIZE OF CHANGE OVER TIME

The comparonomic graph below (Figure 1) represents the fact that King Louis has a more substantial home than us. The exact slope of the line is debatable but the direction, not so much.

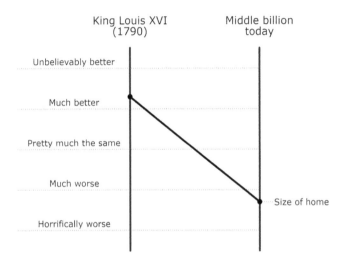

Figure 1 *Comparonomic graph showing the size of the home of King Louis compared to ours today.* Source: *Comparonomics.com.*

For another example, let's compare transport between the two time periods. It is easy to make the comparison because despite King Louis's relative wealth, the fastest way he had to travel was on a horse. A carriage was slower but more comfortable. Compared to modern cars, planes, trains and even bikes, we are doing somewhat better than King Louis. If these modes of transport were shown to King Louis, they would seem unimaginably better, almost like magic. The comparonomic graph (Figure 2) shows how to represent this.

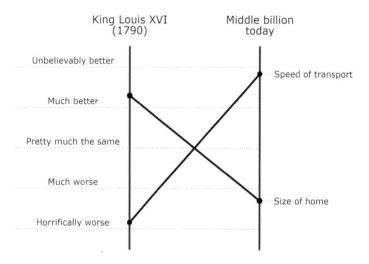

Figure 2 *Comparonomic graph showing the speed of transport is unbelievably better now.* Source: *Comparonomics.com.*

The comparonomic graph is an easy way to show that our transport is faster, but the size of your home is worse than King Louis's. This way we can build up a picture of which things have got better or worse and roughly by how much.

Some things have probably not changed too much. As an example, we probably sleep much the same. I suspect the average person in the 18th century was not as comfortable as we are today, but the King was probably quite comfortable. Figure 3 is an example to show that sleep has perhaps not changed too much over time.

Now let's continue adding comparisons to show how a richer picture can be built up. Consider the state of medical practice (Figure 4). Again, it is easy to show that much of what we take for granted today would be unbelievably better than King Louis had.

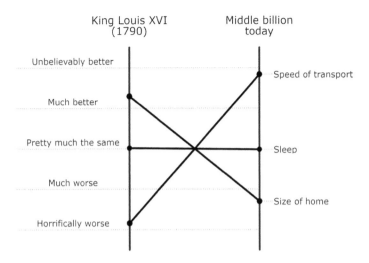

Figure 3 Comparonomic graph showing quality of sleep is much the same. Source: Comparonomics.com.

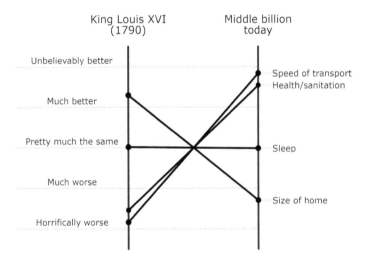

Figure 4 Comparonomic graph that shows health is vastly better now. Source: Comparonomics.com.

Some of the practices in the 18th century we would deem horrifically bad — bloodletting, lead acetate cures, urine for eye infections and opioids to keep the kids calm (this one is at least tempting sometimes maybe).

The last comparison added is social status (Figure 5) to show you can also add non-economic differences on the same sort of graph. Obviously, the King had a higher social status than an average person today.

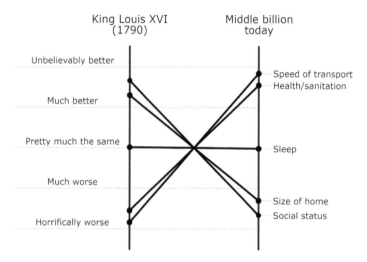

Figure 5 Comparonomic graph showing King Louis had higher social status than most of us. Source: Comparonomics.com.

So, we are building up a way to compare two time periods that are explicit about which bits are better or worse and by roughly how much. Rather than saying King Louis was 1000 times more affluent, you can see what is better and what is worse. In some ways, even an average person now lives better than a king. But more importantly, this is a much clearer model that shows what is different. The model can be built up rapidly by anyone and is a much more useful way to think about how things change.

I am a big believer in the famous quote 'all models are wrong, but some are useful.'[1] The comparonomic graph is more useful for understanding how things change over long time periods where the types of goods and services vary significantly. A more systematic comparison of King Louis's life compared to ours will be developed in the following chapter.

ADDING DETAILS OF HOW THINGS CHANGE

Comparonomic graphs can also dig into particulars of a comparison. If we consider housing (Figure 6), some things are better, and some things are worse than for King Louis.

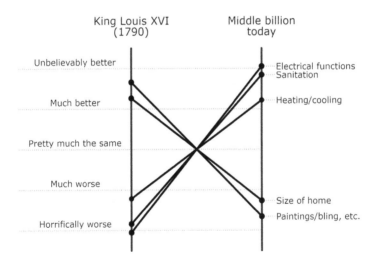

Figure 6 *Comparonomic graph that shows how different aspects of your home compare with King Louis's.* Source: *Comparonomics.com.*

We could debate the various slopes of the lines and the relative importance of these things, but it makes it easy to have such a discussion once you scribble your views on a comparonomic graph. Different people can, and will, have different opinions on this, and that is fine, but it is an easy way to communicate your views.

Apparently one of the reasons for the intricate hedging in the palace of Versailles was to provide excellent places to defecate — not so romantic when you think of the design that way. In summer the palace had a stench of faeces and other smells. I suspect most people would probably opt for a palace over a modern home, but the reality is perhaps a calculus that they could sell it and get a proper contemporary home. Rather than resolving which home is better, the comparonomic graph makes the comparison more open about which bits are better or worse.

The point of this tool is that anyone can compare any two time periods and think about how things have changed. It builds up a picture that can be debated and refined. Saying that a home is more valuable or a person was richer misses details about how things change. Making these beliefs explicit is vital, as the following chapters will show.

COMPARONOMIC GRAPH SUMMARY

The goal of this tool is to allow anyone to create comparisons to explain a rich picture of how they perceive things have changed. It took a surprising amount of time to end up with something this simple and while it may seem trivial now, as you use it in the next chapters hopefully, you will see how powerful it can be.[2]

This tool is also personal so you can make up your mind about what is important to you. It is not about me or any expert telling you how things are but letting you work it out for yourself. It is more compelling in the following chapter when comparonomic graphs analyse how an entire economy changes.

2
HOW DOES YOUR LIFE COMPARE
TO KING LOUIS XVI'S?

IN THIS CHAPTER, I am going to give you complete power to make an economic comparison between any two time periods. It does not rely on data or equations that typically have all sorts of hidden assumptions. I merely ask the following two questions:

- What is important to you?
- How does what you have now compare with what they had in the past?

We will build up a picture based on the comparonomic graph described in the previous chapter, so we can see how things have changed in a more detailed way than a comparison of income levels.

This analysis is not the first one to point out we are better off than King Louis. Matt Ridley[1] explains how specialisation and exchange via markets mean that modern folks have access to vastly more goods and services compared to King Louis. The explanation of specialisation and markets may well be correct, but I will set aside any reason of why things have changed and focus on how they have changed. To keep things relatively simple I have selected seven sectors of the economy that people find important:

- Health/sanitation
- Education/information
- Travel/transportation
- Food/beverage
- Housing
- Entertainment/recreation
- Communication.

In some economies, people spend more directly on these things or via taxes (e.g. health/education). This is not a distinction of interest, just how the quality and quantity of the end product of each of these parts of the economy change.

The list is not claiming to be complete or definitive. The list could be expanded to include clothing, home appliances and professional services but this summary will do for now. Appendix 1 suggests some ways a more comprehensive and definitive picture of the economy can be produced using the same tool.

I have purposefully chosen to mostly use stories to illustrate the differences in each sector of the economy. This makes use of the fact that we seem to have more affinity for stories than data (availability heuristic). Steven Pinker's book,[2]

Enlightenment Now, provides vast quantities of well-researched data that you could also use as a basis for putting together comparonomic graphs.

We will start with comparing our life to King Louis XVI's and then repeat the exercise for comparing ourselves to an average person 50 years ago. The main reason for this is that the first set of comparisons is relatively easy and less debatable. It helps us get used to using the comparonomic graph to describe how things change. As discussed previously, the comparisons we are making when we talk about 'we' is an average person now in a relatively affluent country — the middle billion.

HEALTH/SANITATION

There are large parts of the modern health system that would seem miraculous to King Louis XVI — antibiotics, vaccines, surgeries, scans, and so on. King Louis, it seems, had a good idea of how bad things were back then and delayed what would now be a relatively simple medical procedure. This fear of medicine meant he did not consummate his marriage for nearly 10 years. Let's just say he had some delicate issues in his nether regions that any man now would opt for the most powerful painkillers possible.[3]

As well as the state of curing medical ills, the general sanitation was likely to lead to more illness and would be horrific to modern folks. Patrick Süskind describes it marvellously in the first chapter of *Perfume*:

In the period of which we speak, there reigned in the cities a stench barely conceivable to us modern men and women. The streets stank of manure, the courtyards of urine, the stairwells stank of moldering wood and rat droppings, the kitchens of spoiled cabbage and mutton fat; the unaired parlors stank of stale dust, the bedrooms of greasy sheets, damp featherbeds, and the pungently sweet aroma of chamber pots ..., the whole of the aristocracy stank, even the king himself stank, stank like a rank lion, and the queen like an old goat, summer and winter.[4]

These conditions most of us can avoid these days unless you accidentally wander into a teenager's bedroom. I can't imagine anyone these days wanting to swap their health and sanitation for that of King Louis. Despite his wealth and our relative 'poorness', we can show that our health system and state of medicine is vastly better now (Figure 7).

The slope of the lines I put on the comparonomic graph are subjective, and you are welcome to redraw them with your preferred slope. Go to www.comparonomics.com to use an online tool or print out one. They are simple enough that you don't even need a printout — any pen and paper can be a comparonometer.[5]

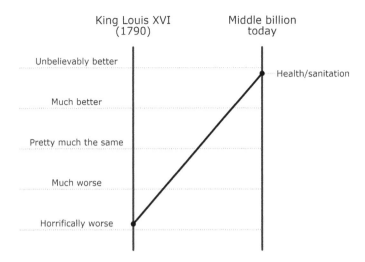

Figure 7 Our health and sanitation is vastly better than King Louis's. Source: Comparonomics.com.

EDUCATION/INFORMATION

The category of education and information combines both what is known and how easy it is to learn these things (Figure 8). The list of things that we know compared to King Louis I'm sure would fall into the category of unimaginable. While it was accepted that the earth was round, the idea that the earth was not the centre of the universe was controversial. No periodic table, electricity, understanding of bacteria, viruses and no Twitter. When it comes to access to information, again you couldn't do anything other than think what we have now would be considered mind-blowingly magical.

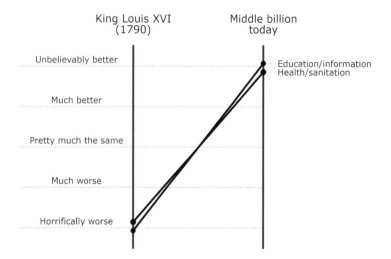

Figure 8 Comparonomic graph that shows Education/information is unbelievably better for us compared to King Louis. Source: *Comparonomics.com.*

TRAVEL

All forms of modern transport are unimaginably better than in the day of King Louis (Figure 9). The obvious example that would seem like magic is air travel but cars and even a new bicycle would seem astonishing. Forcing a modern citizen to use 18th-century transport only would no doubt appear horrifically bad. Enough on travel.

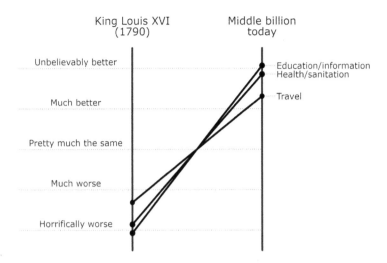

Figure 9 Travel options now are vastly better than for King Louis.
Source: *Comparonomics.com.*

FOOD/BEVERAGE

The comparison for food and beverage is a little more debatable (Figure 10). I've often heard the phrase that a meal 'is fit for a king,' a way of complimenting it. No doubt the King would have eaten exceptionally well for his time, but I suspect he would be blown away walking into a modern supermarket. Louis had no chocolate, ice cream, out-of-season fruit and veges, craft beer, or hundreds of wines from around the world. I would miss a good curry, Caesar salad, hamburger, spaghetti bolognese, guacamole, and sushi. Nope, King Louis had none of that.

Apparently, it took a staggering 498 people to prepare each meal for King Louis.[6] The other thing we take for granted is hygiene of our food. The personal sanitation of the King's

team was horrific by today's standards. Take nearly 500
people with primitive sanitation who didn't know about
washing their hands, and you can be sure he frequently had
a side serving of faeces — King's banquet anyone?

The reason this section is debatable is that King Louis also
misses out on sugar cereal, fizzy drinks, and orange plastic-
wrapped cheese. No doubt these days we make some shitty
'food' but the average person can choose to avoid this if they
wish. I'm guessing if most modern people had the choice for
the rest of their lives of eating and drinking only what King
Louis had or what they have now, they would choose today's
options. In the comparonomic graph below, we can show
that food and beverage have at least got a little better. The
slope is always debatable. My personal opinion is that it has
become much better than shown on this graph, but I'll be
conservative for this example.

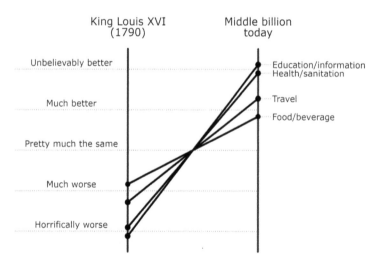

Figure 10 *Food and beverage options are better now than for a king
in 1790.* Source: *Comparonomics.com.*

HOUSING

Housing (Figure 11) is a clear case that King Louis's palaces were, well, ... quite palatial. How cool would it be to live in one of these? It would be much better than the home I live in for sure. But not everything was better. The previous chapter showed how different aspects of housing are better or worse.

Given that size and bling seem important to lots of people, and we take modern things for granted, we will assume that the King's housing was better than ours. There was a curious story of an English couple selling their tiny London apartment and buying a French castle for the same price.[7] This is an option open to anyone, as castles with the level of services equal to King Louis's are inexpensive (no electricity, no toilets, no plumbing, and massive maintenance bills). Anyway, let's assume for this part of the economy, his castle was better than our home.

ENTERTAINMENT/RECREATION

How cool would it be to have your own court jester? Yes, I know this is more of a stereotypical English royal thing but I suspect the reality would get a bit dull after a while. Levels of entertainment and recreation keep getting better. I'm sure the quantity and quality of entertainment and leisure available to us now would blow the socks off Louis XVI (Figure 12).

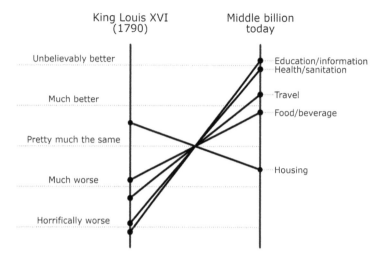

Figure 11 Comparonomic graph that shows our homes are not as good as the King's palaces. Source: Comparonomics.com.

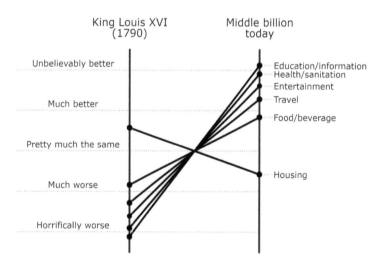

Figure 12 Comparonomic graph that shows entertainment options are dramatically better now. Source: Comparonomics.com.

COMMUNICATION

So why include communication (Figure 13) given it's a tiny part of most economies? Well, the importance of parts of the economy consists of the amount of time we spend on things as well as the amount of money we spend. This way the comparonomic graph can more fully capture all the things we deem essential (see Appendix 1 for more details of this logic).

Progress in communications is straightforward. We mostly have access to as much as we want. We can communicate anywhere in the world at an incremental cost of virtually zero. King Louis would not have believed it. In the pursuit of brevity, I will leave that one there.

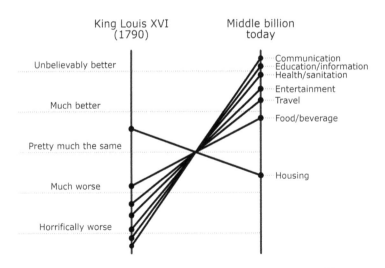

Figure 13 Communications options now are incomprehensibly better. Source: *Comparonomics.com.*

What becomes clear is that even though King Louis was vastly wealthier than the average person now, the quality of things that he had compared to the average person was lousy. A comparison of wealth doesn't do an effective job of analysing how life compares.

SUMMARY OF HOW TO LIVE LIKE A KING

This type of analysis is provocative because if you use conventional economics, then King Louis was vastly wealthier. An inherent assumption in the relative wealth is that he was better off. But this simple analysis shows we are much better off in most ways. More importantly, it is a richer picture of how we think things have changed in magnitude and direction for different parts of what matters to us. There are no hidden assumptions, but like *all* economic models, there is a lot of subjectivity in the analysis. With comparonomic graphs, we expose the subjectivity for everyone to see and open it to debate. If you don't agree that you eat like a king, then you can change the slope and have a good yarn about that comparison. You can even say that you don't care about some things and remove them or add in things important to you that I have left out. The compelling thing about comparonomic graphs is you don't have to rely on experts to tell you how things are — you can think about it and do your own analysis.

The value of a model is not how well it describes the world, but how well it communicates to others how you see the world and how it allows you to understand it. You can then have a discussion and focus on the critical bits you either agree or disagree on.

King Louis was 'richer' than you according to conventional economics, but the comparonomic graph shows this does not mean the same as someone richer than you today. The difference between the two models is as dramatic as being told there is a mountain of wealth when in reality there is a desert of poverty. Many of the King's living conditions would be considered inhumane for a prisoner today (medical, lack of hygiene). Real dollars suck as a measurement when the quality of goods and services changes so dramatically. The point of this example is to show how much a standard economic model can miss. Sure, he was wealthier, but look at how much reducing things to a simple measure of real dollars can overlook.

The comparison to a king from hundreds of years ago is a little trivial but it was surprising to me how dramatically better we live than King Louis XVI.

3

WHY COMPARONOMIC GRAPHS
ARE IMPORTANT AND USEFUL

THE SIMPLE EXAMPLE of comparing our life to King Louis's shows how bad constant dollar income is for understanding change over time. The standard economic analysis would show Louis was thousands of times wealthier in 'real dollars' but I doubt anyone would want to swap when they understand the reality of his life.

In just a few minutes, anyone with no knowledge of economics can create a model to describe how life compares. The comparonomic graph is more useful than standard economic tools for comparing long time periods where the types of goods and services fundamentally change. If we don't accurately understand how things have changed in the past, we have little hope of understanding what we could do to make things better. Comparonomic graphs highlight three crucial messages:

- Relative income is a feeble measure to compare how well off people are over time periods when the things available are dramatically different.
- You can build a more useful, detailed and accurate understanding of how things change compared to professional economists who are using inappropriate tools. You don't need a PhD in economics to be able to understand, build and communicate using comparonomic graphs.
- A better understanding of how things have changed could be useful for understanding what's going on in the world today.

WHEN IS COMPARONOMICS USEFUL AND WHEN IS IT NOT?

I am not proposing throwing out conventional economic modelling because constant wages/income is appropriate for short-term measurements from quarter to quarter. The example above shows how hopeless constant dollars are as a comparison over the long term. I suspect that constant dollar comparisons will get worse where the rate of change of things is accelerating as appears to be happening with modern technologies.

A comparonomic graph would be useless comparing one quarter to another — every line would be flat. But for long-term analysis, it is much more insightful. My guess is that a comparonomic graph needs at least 10–20 years' time difference to be useful.

Figure 14 shows standard economics is most useful when there is a relatively low change in the type of goods and services available (short time periods). When the types of products and services change dramatically (extended time periods), then comparonomic graphs are more useful. When there is a low change in types of goods and services, comparonomic graphs are next to useless.

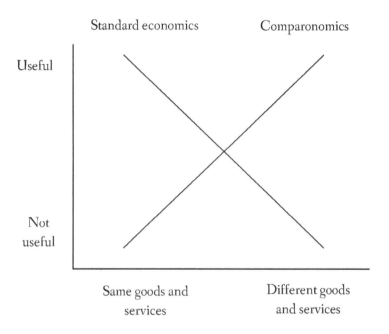

Figure 14 When different economic models are most useful and least useful.

For long time periods, comparonomic graphs are useful and standard economics models less useful. One factor that could be compelling is that the rate of change of goods and services available seems to be changing faster now than previously, so comparonomic graphs could be getting more useful for shorter time periods.

Rather than saying comparonomics is right and conventional economics is wrong, I'd prefer to say comparonomics seems a lot more useful than traditional economics for long-term time comparisons. Conventional analysis methods miss so many things that are important to us.

HOW TO MATHEMATISE COMPARONOMICS

It could be argued that a comparonomic graph is not as accurate or useful as standard economics tools because there is no 'science', usually assumed to mean numbers that we can verify. Well, you can mathematise this analysis by doing the following things:

- The importance of different parts of the economy can be measured by looking in aggregate at how much time and/or money we spend on different sectors of the economy.
- The rate of improvement can be measured by looking at the length of time it takes for something we deem important to go from impossible to obtain to being available to everyone. To create an easy measurement for this, we can measure the time it takes for a product or service to go from only available to the 10% wealthiest to being accessible to 90% of the people. If it takes 100 years for plumbing to go from 10% of people to 90%, then it is a lower rate of growth than smartphones, taking only 10 years.
- These numbers could be aggregated to calculate an

overall figure for the value of goods and services from one period to another. This can determine what we call the Speed of Economic Progress (SEP), which is an alternative measure of economic growth comparable to GDP.

I have expanded how this could lead to a new form of economic growth theory in Appendix 1. I put this in an appendix as I don't want to complicate the core narrative of this book. As discussed previously I am purposefully producing a high-level sketch of a broad picture rather than a detailed painting.

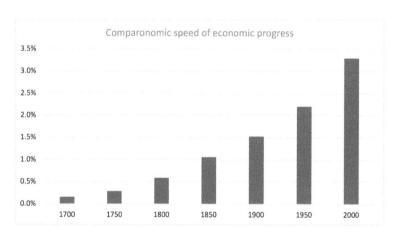

Figure 15 The speed of economic progress appears to be getting faster over time.

Figure 15 is a graph that shows the speed of economic progress is increasing faster now than ever before. The numbers in the chart are a rough analysis but indicate that, if anything, the rate at which new goods and services make it to the whole population is accelerating. Notice I didn't say economic growth is accelerating as this has a precise alternative definition. The speed of economic progress considers the fact that the types of goods and services important to us change over time. The speed of economic progress is the relative speed with which everyone gets goods and services that used to be available to only the rich. The speed of economic progress certainly seems to be accelerating, and I would imagine most people would interpret this as a good thing.

Numbers don't necessarily mean speed of economic progress is more scientific or more useful than a comparonomic graph. I could run an 'objective' mathematical version of the comparonomic model to show that we are 26.24[1] times wealthier than King Louis (the opposite result of what constant dollar analysis would show). Even though this may be more mathematical and 'verifiable', it is not necessarily an insightful model compared to a comparonomic graph where the assumptions and differences between sectors are open to see. The comparonomic graph is more accessible for anyone to participate and therefore easier to scrutinise, tweak, debate or accept. The assumptions and differences in rates of change are plain to see and not wrapped up in some falsely worshipped, mathematically precise number.

Imagine an alternative way of being introduced to comparonomics by reading an article that may have the title 'New economic theory' shows that we are 26.2 times richer than King Louis XVI' (news titles with 'economic theory' are hardly common and will never win a clickbait contest). Your gut reaction to this new information could include thoughts of 'This doesn't seem right — King Louis had a couple of huge palaces and servants on tap. Most people I know are struggling. Sounds like some ivory tower theory of no use to me.' I will get on to why we feel like we are struggling later but, hopefully, you can follow the logic of comparonomic graphs and agree that by most measures we are much better off than King Louis. Because there are no numbers in the comparonomic graph, it doesn't make it any less useful or even any less scientific.

It is worth emphasising here how different the results are from conventional economics that show King Louis is vastly wealthier than us. The reality is that many aspects of his life were more horrific than how we treat a dog. This result is so different from the commonly accepted wisdom that there should be scepticism — make your own graph and see what you think. There is nothing inherently optimistic about the tool. Try comparing Zimbabwe to 30 years ago, and you can see there is nothing about the tool that is optimistic. I ask two simple questions:

- What is important to you?
- How do levels of goods and services compare?

The conclusions about the inadequacy of conventional economic tools are too significant to let experts debate over the next 20 years before they become commonly understood. Also, I cannot think of any other area of life where such a simple, clean analysis can show how limited currently accepted models are.

While comparonomic graphs are not difficult to understand, they are a much more open and sophisticated way of thinking about change. Now that you can use the tool, let's look at a more useful and intriguing comparison. How does the life of the middle billion compare now to 50 years ago? The early 1970s were considered a golden age by some, so let's plunge in and make a comparison.

4
HOW DOES OUR LIFE COMPARE
TO 50 YEARS AGO?

THE COMPARISON with King Louis in the 18th century was easy because many of the things we have now were not available then. It is a little more debatable to make the comparison to the early 1970s but let's start building up a picture. With the stories in the chapter, don't focus too much on them being precisely 50 years ago but around that time.

As a reminder, the method for building up the picture is to rattle off some stories about the difference between the two time periods and put a line on the comparonomic graph. I purposefully try to illustrate not with data but stories, so they are memorable. Other authors have done a sensational job of putting together hard-core data that highlight this same progress. If you prefer this form of evidence, I'd recommend Steven Pinker's book *Enlightenment Now: The Case for Reason, Science, Humanism, and Progress,* or websites like ourworldindata.org or humanprogress.org.

The slope of the line on comparonomic graphs is always debatable, but the direction typically isn't. Don't get too hung up on the exact gradient of the line, as it is subjective. Feel free to make your own version of the comparonomic graph as you go through the chapter (www.comparonomics.com).

In the examples below, I purposefully pick some of the most dramatic examples and stories to illustrate how much things have changed. This is not a proof that everything has got better, but there does seem to be a consistently positive trend in many things. Also, keep in mind that in the next chapter I will list an extensive range of genuine reasons why we don't *feel* so good about how things have changed.

In these examples, I never talk about price, cost, or affordability because there are so many embedded assumptions in the way these things are defined. I ask, 'What was it like 50 years ago for the middle billion and what is it like now?' Would you swap what they had on average with what we have on average now? How strongly do you feel is the difference?

HEALTH

Below is a list of facts comparing health and medicine from 50 years ago:

- The link between smoking and poor health was not widely accepted. It was not that long since the Flintstones were advertising cigarettes and beer.
- Cancer survival rates were half what they are now.

- Since then, thousands of procedures and medicines have been invented or improved.
- Pacemakers and heart surgery have gone from being rare and expensive to ordinary and accepted as not such a big deal.
- There were protests on the street about the first IVF fertility treatments but they are standard now, and we don't think twice about them.
- A hip replacement is considered one of the most life-transforming procedures, adding years of quality to later life. It's not uncommon to hear complaints about the cost of hip replacements or delays in getting them but remember no one had them 50 years ago (not even kings).
- Shoving a pickaxe up your nose to mush up part of your brain had only recently been banned as medical treatment. The inventor of frontal lobotomy even got a Nobel Prize.
- The speed of development of treatments and vaccines for pandemics is dramatically better. We are likely to always have outbreaks of infectious disease and from a medical point of view it's much better to have the medical tools we have now. There is no better time in history for Covid-19 to turn up.

This topic can be emotionally challenging because it is so easy to jump to the question of how broken, unfair or expensive current health care is. We probably have strong views on the reasons health is costly or unjust and why different countries have better systems. It's normal to have strong opinions on these things but they are irrelevant for this analysis. Put them to one side and compare the level of service for the middle billion now and 50 years ago.

It is also hard not to jump into the question of how health is likely to change in the future. There is significant evidence for flattening of life expectancy possibly due to obesity, and our collective health could decline. Or if you believe the optimists we are on the verge of solving old age with new technologies. Both things I purposefully put to one side because they are about guessing why things change or what is going to happen in the future. Let's focus on the state of health for the average person now compared to 50 years ago (Figure 16).

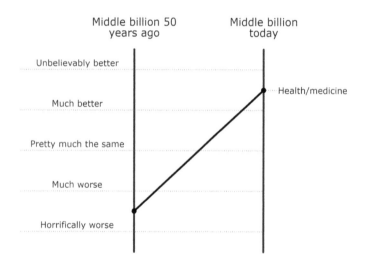

Figure 16 *Health and medicine are much better now than 50 years ago. Source: Comparonomics.com.*

If someone could offer you a health system in which the average person lived 10–15 years longer, you would find that offer unbelievably better. If health becomes so bad the average life expectancy goes down by 10–15 years, you would probably find that horrifically bad. There is no question our state of health/medicine is vastly better than 50 years ago, and it is a personal judgement as to the slope of the line.

EDUCATION/INFORMATION

Education and information are grouped together because it is a combination of how much you know and how easy it is to know it (Figure 17). It is probably easy to sit back and think education was better in the good old days. Below are a few facts on things we didn't know, and facts about how easy it is to get access to information compared to 50 years ago:

- We didn't know about global warming — in fact, we worried about an ice age.
- We thought putting lead in fuel was a good thing but were poisoning the general population.
- If you wanted to find out something, you would head off to the library — there were no search engines. As much as we complain about alternative facts, it is easy to forget how much less rubbish people can spout on about these days. Most things that sound dodgy we can immediately fact-check. The record number of children by one woman — 69? Yep — easy to check. It rains diamonds on Saturn. Cambridge University is older than Aztec civilisation. Quick as a flash easy to find out and check almost anything. There are significant

problems with 'fake' news too, but it seems most
can tell the difference.

- It is possible that because of smartphones, we have
faster, more accurate access to information than the
most powerful person in the world when Bill
Clinton was president.

If you could offer today's access to information to someone
from 50 years ago, they would be astonished. It would seem
like magic. Try getting anyone to do research for a project
and take the internet from them. It seems horrifically
primitive having to use microfiche at the library.

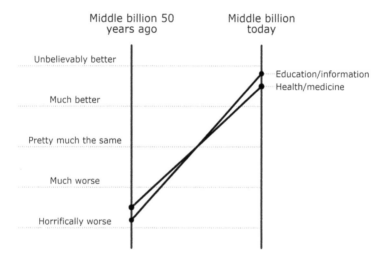

Figure 17 The state of Education/information is much better now.
Source: *Comparonomics.com.*

One of my favourite examples of this is how in some
countries it is now considered a fundamental human right to
have broadband internet access.[1] Well, you know the

wealthiest billionaire in the world didn't have it 15 years ago. Things go from impossible to fundamental human right in the blink of an eye. You could only draw a very steep line to describe the progress we have made in this part of the economy.

TRAVEL

Travel is something that has not changed too much in the core functionality for the last 50 years (Figure 18). Our main ways of getting around are still cars, bikes, trains, and airplanes. There is a vast amount of evidence that all these forms are used more frequently and are of higher quality:

- Air travel has gone from a novel luxury to a mundane thing that most of the middle billion would do reasonably regularly.[2]
- Average cars now have air-con, fuel efficiency, airbags, and seatbelts.[3] They are vastly more reliable, and the days of keeping water, oil, and tools for fixing your car are mostly gone.
- Bikes have disc brakes, suspension, gear options galore but still have those lovely bells.
- Apps make public transport vastly easier in a modern city. Options for train, bus, walking, Uber or any combinations are easy to see.
- Even a good weather app can make the choice of walking more likely to turn out well.
- You were two to eight times more likely to die in a car crash 50 years ago (depending on where you are from).[4]

- You were six times more likely to die in an airplane crash 50 years ago.[5]
- But we also have congestion, airport security checks, and associated hassles.

I doubt anyone would swap accessibility of flights and functions of cars for versions from 50 years ago. Transport is much better now but probably not unbelievable. I suspect driverless cars and even flying vehicles are set to transform the safety and price of travel even further, but that is irrelevant for this discussion given our agreement to refrain from speculating on the future. Would you give up modern transport for that of 50 years ago?

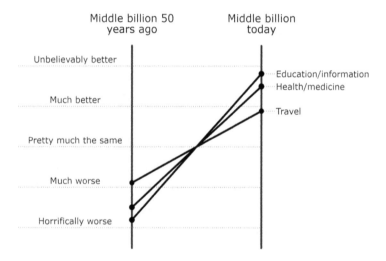

Figure 18 *Travel options and safety are much better now.* Source: *Comparonomics.com.*

COMMUNICATION

As discussed earlier, communication (Figure 19) would not typically be an economic sector of a similar size to housing and health. One of the points of this analysis is that it is not the dollar size of an economic sector but also how much time we spend using it.

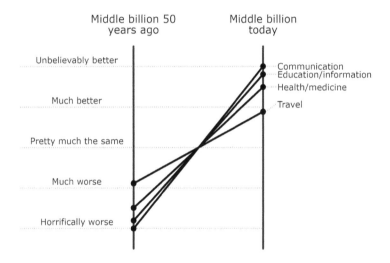

Figure 19 Communication options these days are unbelievably better. Source: *Comparonomics.com.*

Our daily life is full with the use of communication tools that would be considered unbelievable to anyone 50 years ago. Take a simple telephone call. Sure, they had them, but now they are next to free from anywhere. Then there is the amount of time we spend on email, texting and all the wonders of a smartphone. An analysis of the latest iPhone compared it to its performance with 1957 technology:[6]

- Cost 150 trillion of today's dollars: one and a half times today's global annual product
- Drawn 150 terawatts of power—30 times the world's current generating capacity.

You can only draw a very steep line to show the progress of communication tools and services over the last 50 years.

FOOD/BEVERAGE

Food and beverage have probably not changed as dramatically for the average person in the last 50 years (Figure 20). There is almost certainly an extensive range of things a time traveller would miss about what we have now. Remember for simplicity's sake the top 10% and bottom 10% of people are excluded from this analysis. How have things changed for the middle billion?

- How has the quality of coffee changed over 50 years?
- I remember cask wine came in two main types, red or white.
- Look at some cooking books or food magazines from the early 1970s. Very few magazines and obviously no blogs.
- The term 'foodie' didn't appear until the 1980s.
- Lettuce used to mean iceberg — what else was there?
- Bland white bread was often the norm.
- Cheese came in big blocks, and the cheese options at most stores now would seem unknown to

someone from the 1970s (unless you were in parts of Europe, of course).

- I remember hearing about the odd practice of eating raw fish as a child. This seemed exotic and a little crazy but now it is a familiar food option for much of the middle billion.
- We eat out much more often than 50 years ago and my guess is that restaurant food quality is vastly better in general.
- These is some evidence that average nutrition values of food have fallen[7] but it is hard to tell for sure given the poor test and data from 50 years ago.
- We do know they used large quantities of chemicals in the past that are now banned. As an example, in early 1970s they were still using 40,000 tons of DDT annually. You would struggle to get organic food even if you wanted to.
- Food labelling was mostly non-existent 50 years ago so you often didn't know what additives were in the food purchased.

One of the best ways to think about how this has changed is to ask yourself, if you had the choice of food and beverage now compared to what was on offer to the middle billion 50 years ago, what would you choose? And then how strongly you feel about that, to put a slope on the line. I look at a lot of the foods I love now that were not as freely available — sushi, avocados, cos lettuce, craft beer, French-style cheese, wholegrain breads, gourmet sausages, boned chicken, fresh herbs and ethnic food options. You may have a different view on things, and that's fine. The questions are 'What is important to you?' and 'How has this changed?'

For this sector of the economy, I've put a moderately sloped line to show that food and beverage have improved but not as much as other sectors of the economy.

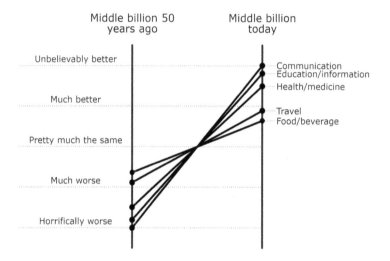

Figure 20 Modern food and beverage seem to be better. Source: *Comparonomics.com.*

HOUSING

Housing (Figure 21) is something that probably has not changed dramatically on average. The size of the average house has increased significantly in some countries (e.g. US, Australia) but not as much in Asia and Europe. The building regulations in most countries have moved on so much that a typical home built 50 years ago would be illegal to build now. Usual improvements these days include insulation, double glazing, safety (smoke alarms, wiring, handrails), less toxicity (no lead pipes), fire-retardant materials, soundproofing, water ingress protection and better lighting.

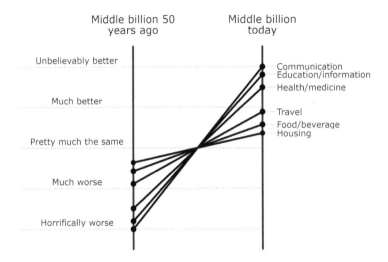

Figure 21 *Average housing is better than 50 years ago.* Source: *Comparonomics.com.*

Modern homes also now include a vast number of products that would have appeared magic to many 50 years ago: dishwashers, microwaves, waste disposal, ice makers, air-conditioning,[8] flat-screen TVs, hooded barbecues, power tools, awnings, decks, garage door openers, security systems, and automatic lights.[9] While there is enormous pressure on housing affordability in some of the most desirable cities, it has not changed so much for most of the middle billion. But hold on, 50 years ago people could buy a house on just one income and now you really need two incomes so surely we are worse off? This a reflection that the average household now has two incomes. With mobile skilled populations all wanting to live in the most desirable places, this certainly drives up prices making it less affordable for many and this adds to the sense of struggle. This particular topic is different from comparing the average house people live in now to 50 years ago.

It seems that people prefer the modern home because that is what they choose. If you have a home from 50 years ago, it has typically been upgraded to include many of the modern features such as decent bathrooms, kitchen and insulation. Even given all these improvements, I've only got a gentle slope to show that housing has got better. If anything, it should probably be steeper.

ENTERTAINMENT/RECREATION

It may feel like we no longer have enough downtime for recreation and entertainment (Figure 22), but data shows that the middle billion probably have more free time than ever[10]. So how has the quality of entertainment and recreation changed?

- 50 years ago, most TVs were still black and white and tiny by today's standards.
- Four to five channels if you were lucky,[11] compared with thousands of on-demand options available now.[12]
- No portable music options other than radio — even cassettes were not available. We now have millions of song options available instantly.
- Exercise options were limited and even jogging wasn't a commonly known word or thing.

- No mountain biking, BMX, windsurfing, paddle boarding or skateboarding — there was line dancing though.
- Book/magazine selection was limited to your local store or library.
- We now have thousands of talks from world experts on any topic of interest at your fingertips.

While some of these entertainment options are a matter of trend, I suspect that no one would want to give up what we have today, and anyone from 50 years ago would struggle to believe the options we have now.

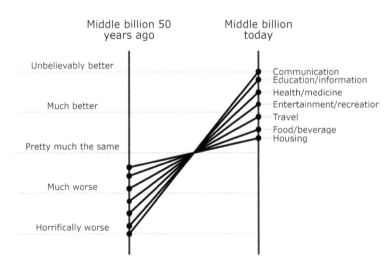

Figure 22 Entertainment is vastly better now compared to 50 years ago. All aspects of the economy are significantly better these days and some parts dramatically better. Source: Comparonomics.com.

SUMMARY OF HOW THE AVERAGE PERSON IS GETTING ON AFTER 50 YEARS

You would have to summarise life compared to 50 years ago as dramatically better by all of these measures. This may seem at odds with your gut feel for how things have changed, and it is different from what some economic models tell us. Before dismissing outright the idea that things are better, check out Part Two of this book, which explains why we feel gloomy, and come back to this analysis.

> The economist Don Boudreaux imagined the average American time-travelling back to 1967 with his modern income. He might be the richest person in town, but no amount of money could buy him the delights of eBay, Amazon, Starbucks, Wal-Mart, Prozac, Google.[13]

Because progress has been good to date, this is no guarantee it will go on forever. Nicholas Taleb described the story of a turkey in his book *The Black Swan*.[14]

> Consider a turkey that is fed every day. Every single feeding will firm up the bird's belief that it is the general rule of life to be fed every day by friendly members of the human race 'looking out for its best interests,' as a politician would say. 'On the afternoon of the Wednesday before Thanksgiving, something unexpected will happen to the turkey. It will incur a revision of belief.

None of this analysis precludes the possibility of some significant change in trends. However, the changes outlined in the comparonomic graphs ride over the top of many black swan events like the global financial crises, 9/11, and the fall of the Berlin Wall. Even if you believe things are about to collapse dramatically, it is still no excuse for not acknowledging the consistent progress we have made lately on a whole range of things. This book is not speculating about the future, just trying to agree on what has happened so far, which seems to be mostly good news.

HOW CONVENTIONAL ECONOMICS VIEWS THE LAST 50 YEARS

There is a prevailing thought that for a lot of people, there has been minimal improvement in real wages since the 1970s. Most of the increase in wealth has gone to the top 1–10%, and much of the 'middle class' or poorer people are not much better off. Two graphs (Figures 23 and 24) [15,16] are typical of the economics charts that show stagnant wages for 50 years.

'For most workers, real wages have barely budged for decades.'[17] There are so many assumptions tied up in the statement that it is hard to know where to start unpacking it. I am not going to comment on the mountain of literature that discusses in detail the pros and cons of the assumptions and details. One of the reasons I don't even try is that the discussion quickly gets so academic that it is not easy for most people to participate in so they disengage. Meticulously researched details count for a lot less when what it measures is so hopelessly flawed. With a comparonomic graph, anyone can participate and build their

own view and have a richer, more believable personal view
of how things have changed.

Americans' paychecks are bigger than 40 years ago, but their purchasing power has hardly budged

Average hourly wages in the U.S., seasonally adjusted

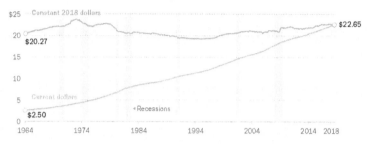

Figure 23 Conventional economics indicates that the purchasing power of wages is flat over the last 50 years. Chart source: *Pew Research Center*

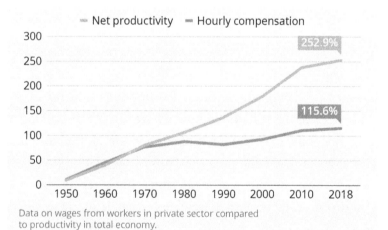

Data on wages from workers in private sector compared to productivity in total economy.

Figure 24 Conventional economics shows wages falling behind productivity growth for 50 years. Chart source: *Statista.*

The elephant graph (Figure 25)[18] highlights some significant differences in income growth over time, although only going back to 1988 rather than 50 years ago. The great news is that lots of low-income people's incomes are growing rapidly and they are leaping out of extreme poverty. It also highlights how much the top few percent have been booming too. There is obviously some progress to be made to help the poorest people, which probably should be the main conclusion from the graph. The key thing some focus on is how little 'growth' there has been in the developed world middle class — there is even comment that this means the middle class is in decline.

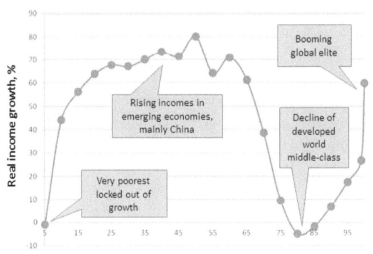

Figure 25 *Normal economic measures show the decline of the middle billion — or that is the story that is told.*

A wide range of economic models do not show things are as bad as flat growth or decline. However, it seems that this opinion that life used to be better has made it into public perception.

> In a 2015 survey, 70% of Britons agreed with the statement that 'things are worse than they used to be,' even though at the time Britons were in fact 'richer, healthier and longer-living than ever before.'[19]

> First time in history — average Americans have less education and are less prosperous than their parents.[20]

> 1974 would mark a fundamental breakpoint in American economic history. In the years since, the tide has continued to rise, but a growing number of boats have been chained to the bottom.[21]

There is even a term for this called declinism[22] — the belief that a society or institution is tending towards decline. This is primarily attributed to the cognitive bias called rosy retrospection or nostalgia bias and leads to viewing the past favourably and the future negatively. In the following chapters, I flesh out a broader range of quirks in perception that led us to a pessimistic view of current life.

The gloomy economic conclusions reflect in public perception. Pew Research asked 'Life in our country today is _____ than it was 50 years ago for people like me.'[23] Half thought better, half worse. Notably, lots of countries in the middle billion thought things were worse. This sense of despondency about progress has made its way into the public psyche sufficiently that it is commonly believed to influence genuine public opinion and politics. You can't 'Make America Great Again' if it was actually worse in the past.

One of the most prominent economists[24] expressing the view that economic growth has fallen is Robert J. Gordon. Part of his argument is that the significant problems are solved already — health, sanitation, transport, and food. There will probably never be leaps like that again and, in some ways, I agree with this. Now the middle billion have mostly solved famine, plagues, and war, everything else is trivial. The big problems in life are solved for the middle billion. Where I disagree is that somehow this means things are broken. How can this be anything other than great news? Robert Gordon's book about the decline of economic growth was also one of the things that accelerated the writing of this book. His pessimistic interpretation of life's progress needs to be challenged.

I am completely out of sync with many other economists on how they see declining productivity. A paper by Bloom et al.[25] uses the example of Moore's Law getting harder as proof of falling productivity. A section of the economy that has got millions of times cheaper and faster over 50 years has a problem with productivity ... I'm sorry but if your house got a million times cheaper you would be thrilled. All I can say is they have, what is to me, an odd way of thinking about the way things get better over time.

THE MIDDLE BILLION IS THE 1% FROM A HISTORICAL PERSPECTIVE

Historically, an estimated 100 billion people have existed over history. It seems clear that the middle billion are better off than the other 99 billion that have ever existed, and better off by a vast margin. It is a great time to have been born and, from a historic perspective, you are the wealthiest 1%. You are the 1%! It is better than being in the 1% any time in the past because the average person has way more things that were impossible for even kings. I'd estimate that about half the time we use goods or services, they are better than the wealthiest person in the world 50 years ago.

CHAPTER CONCLUSIONS

The goal of this chapter was to show how you can create mini thought experiments to gauge how well off you are compared to any time in the past. It is not about my telling you how things are but giving you a tool so you can work it out yourself. The results of significant progress in all sectors seem at odds with the results from conventional economic analysis that implies many of us are not doing much better than 50 years ago.

It is important to note that there is nothing inherently optimistic about this tool. Comparing these same things over the last 20 years in Venezuela is not going to produce a comparonomic graph showing things have got better.

So how does standard economics miss such huge improvements? All the possible explanations have pros and cons but I want to skip the why and move on to the even more perplexing question: Given things have got much better, why don't we feel any better? Maybe economic productivity is not broken — economic measurement and what we aim for is broken.

The reason this is so important is that if we don't accurately understand how things are changing, we have little hope of doing things that are likely to make things better. Imagine being in a car and wanting to go faster. If the speedo says you are slowing down, but the speedo is broken, then it is not much use for helping you drive. What I am proposing is to look out the window and see progress for ourselves rather than rely on inappropriate, broken measurement tools.

Hopefully, after this chapter, you will be feeling good about how well off you are compared to even kings or our disco, flared-trouser-wearing 1970s friends. However, maybe the reason we feel so frustrated about progress is that society is falling apart. We all know how bad some of the social trends in modern society are ... well, we can use the same comparonomic graph tool to delve into how social patterns are changing too.

5
CHANGES IN SOCIAL TRENDS

THE PREVIOUS CHAPTER analysed how we are progressing economically and this chapter examines how things are developing socially. Maybe the reason we feel so bad is that society is falling to pieces in other dimensions?

The creation of comparonomic graphs in this chapter is a little more subjective for a couple of reasons. The first is that the changes are, in general, more subjective and open for debate depending on your worldview. The second is that even the direction of change and whether that is good or not is subjective.

CHANGES IN SOCIAL TRENDS ARE SUBJECTIVE

First, we must agree how a social pattern has changed and then whether the change is in a positive direction. We can all agree that society's acceptance of non-heterosexual behaviour has become much more prevalent. It was illegal in most places back in the 1970s. Many folks now think persecuting people based on who they love is an inappropriate thing. However, if you are at the edge of some religious groups, this acceptance of immoral behaviour is considered a horrific, scary, plummeting of moral standards. The Ku Klux Klan will not view decreased racism positively, whereas most of us think it is a great thing. For many folks, the fact that women are treated more fairly than in the past is a good thing. However, from the ISIS caliphate's perspective, more rights for women is a bad thing and they have chosen to fix it by actions that many of us would see as making matters worse. Whether a change is good or not is a value judgment that we want to make explicit. If you are of the view that we should treat arbitrary subsections of the population as second-class citizens, then you will probably struggle with this chapter (probably the whole book, actually).

Even reduction in violence is a subjective thing. When I went to school, if a teacher got mad at you, they took you out the back and whacked you with a stick (not me, of course, given my angelic tendencies). This seems comically barbaric now but there are still those who hark back to the good old days of 'proper' discipline. Some states persist with the ultimate form of violence of killing citizens if they have been bad enough. Most nations have reduced violence but those who think the death penalty and hitting children is okay probably believe the trend of this reduction in violence is a bad thing. It is worth noting that even if your views on the change in the trend are different from other people, you can state that and use a comparonomic graph to illustrate it. The tool is not inherently biased but makes your view and assumptions explicit and open to debate. For each line in the comparonomic graph, we need to make three judgments:

- How has the social trend changed?
- Is the direction of change a good or bad thing?
- How much has it changed — what is the slope of the graph?

Why it matters is that rather than saying 'morals have collapsed' or 'family values are much worse', you can be explicit about how you think things have changed and whether the change is a good or a bad thing. Examples could include 'I think there is less racism now and this is a good thing' or 'I think acceptance of the LGBT community has increased, and this is a bad thing.'[1]

The list of things chosen to discuss is a small subset of everything that could be significant. Again, this list is not comprehensive or definitive but an example selection. Let us think about how the following social trends have changed over time:

- Sexism
- Intelligence
- Economic inequality
- Violence
- Sexual freedom (e.g. homophobia)
- Racism
- Social status.

Other topics that could have been included are political/religious freedom, environment, freedom of speech or acceptance of hipster beards. Some are trivial, and others could fill a whole book, e.g. trends in the environment. You can choose to explore any of these topics as well by asking:

- Which social trends are important to me?
- How have they changed over time?
- Is the change positive or negative?

In the graphs below, I assume that racism, sexism, and homophobia are undesirable and there are merits to not labelling people and persecuting them for their differences. This is not a universal opinion, but you are welcome to sketch your own version.

SOCIETY IN 18TH-CENTURY FRANCE

In this section, I will brush over changes quickly as it seems undebatable how many social changes there have been since the time of King Louis in the 18th century. I will spend more time digging into the details of social trends from 50 years below. First, a quick list of comments on social trends from the days of King Louis:

- Sexism — men were top of the pile and women had little say in the running of society. I wanted to emphasise this by saying women had no voting rights but many men didn't get to vote either! Females' primary role in life was to find a man and raise a family.

- Intelligence — the 'Flynn effect' shows that people are more intelligent over time at least by easily measurable IQ tests. If we assume that King Louis was a lot smarter than average for his day, he would almost be considered intellectually disabled by today's standards.[2]
- Racism — French aristocracy was involved in slave trading in colonies and there were widespread anti-Semitic attitudes.[3]
- Economic inequality — inequalities all around Europe at that time were dramatically worse compared to today, but the level of difference in France was extreme with people dying of starvation while outside the gates of vast, grand palaces. It is not hard to sympathise with why a revolution was brewing.
- Violence — Steven Pinker's book *The Better Angels of Our Nature* has a vast trove of data on how violent life was even for kings. King Louis had a date with the guillotine just around the corner so the threat was more than academic.
- Social status — King Louis was the absolute top of the social standings so there is no doubt that this is one thing where he was doing way better than the middle billion today.
- Sexual freedom (e.g. homophobia) — being homosexual was a capital offence.

For speed of analysis, all the lines on the comparonomic graph are put on at once (Figure 26). The slopes of the lines are debatable, but the direction seems clear.

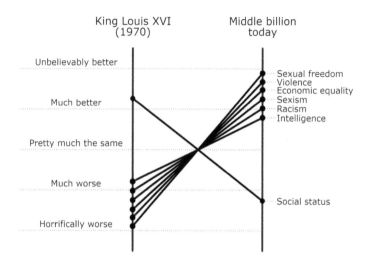

Figure 26 Most social trends are dramatically better now compared to King Louis's time. Source: Comparonomics.com.

At a high level, it seems many things we consider important are much better now than they were for King Louis XVI. The obvious thing Louis had that we can't all have is social status. More on social status later.

In a few minutes and with one comparonomic graph, you can explicitly show the direction and size of how you think complex social factors have changed between two time periods. Feel free to draw your own version.

SOCIAL TRENDS OVER THE LAST 50 YEARS

In each of the sections below, there is a more in-depth discussion of the social trends over the previous 50 years.

SEXISM

We all know how bad sexism is around the world and the many things we need to do to improve it. Below are a few stories to put in perspective how 50 years ago it was even worse. There are mountains of statistics about why there is more equality now, like the increasing percentage of female doctors and lawyers who graduate.[4] Instead of listing statistics, I'll put a few examples of things that are jaw-droppingly sexist by today's standards.

- In Switzerland, some women were not allowed to vote.
- In the US, women were not allowed to apply for a credit card without their husband's permission.[5]
- It was acceptable to fire women who got pregnant.
- Women were not allowed to run in marathons — presumably to protect them from too much strain.
- No woman had led an OECD country (now many have[6]).
- The term 'sexual harassment' was not coined until 1975. Not because it didn't happen but probably because it was a normal and accepted part of life.
- In the US, it was perfectly legal to rape your wife as much as you liked.

As is obvious from the Me Too movement, we have a long way to go when it comes to sexism, but we have also made a lot of progress in the last 50 years. Some countries have yet to make the full step to democracy where women are deemed fit to have a turn leading. Others have had many female leaders, so it's barely a talking point.

The only way to interpret the trend is that there has been a significant change (Figure 27). Explicitly, I am going to say that the transformation has been in a positive direction while acknowledging that some people would argue that is not the case. They would likely be a minority.

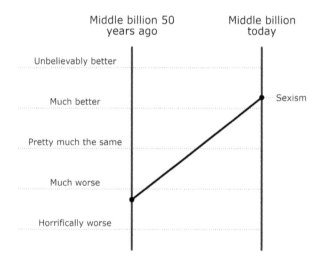

Figure 27 Sexism was much worse 50 years ago. Source: *Comparonomics.com.*

INTELLIGENCE

I have included changes in intelligence to show that you can demonstrate a range of different types of changes in society on a comparonomic graph (Figure 28). The Flynn effect[7] probably seems counterintuitive to most people but there is a significant body of evidence to suggest that we are consistently getting smarter by two or three IQ points per decade. IQ is not necessarily the only form of intelligence but is included here as it is easily measured and an example of other factors that can be included in comparisons.

The reasons for the IQ improvement range from better schooling, to more stimulating environments, to better nutrition and even less inbreeding (it would be impolite to mention some places where this may not be the case). It is hard to ignore the reasons for why things change but I am going to focus on the fact that there have been significant improvements in intelligence. This means that 50 years ago the average person would be around 10–15 IQ points lower. Harking back to the good old days means wishing we were significantly duller.

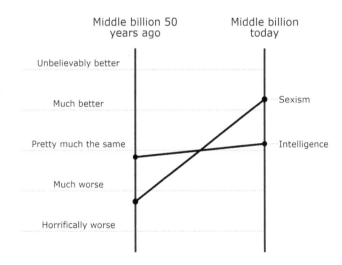

Figure 28 We are even a bit smarter than 50 years ago. Source: *Comparonomics.com.*

ECONOMIC INEQUALITY

There is growing evidence on rising inequality in the world, and in the last 50 years there has been a significant increase particularly in the OECD countries that form the middle billion.[8] I defined our middle billion as not including the top and bottom 10% of the income population, so this has probably changed less for this group. Later I explore the role of inequality in some detail on how it affects our thoughts on progress.

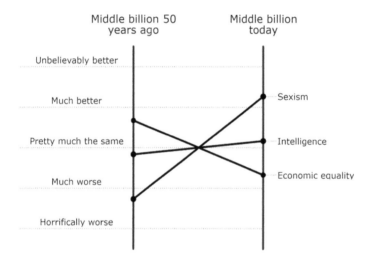

Figure 29 *Economic inequality has got worse over the last 50 years.*
Source: *Comparonomics.com.*

I am also keen to include at least something in the comparonomic graph to demonstrate that not everything has improved (Figure 29). There are plenty of people who would see increasing inequality as a good thing rather than a bad thing.[9] My job here is not to judge. If you think economic inequality is good, feel free to draw your own version with the lines going the way you think they should.

It does seem that Piketty's[10] work along with Stiglitz[11] and many others is increasing the perception that rising inequality is a problem. Let's assume for argument's sake this is a bad thing. Again, the slope of the line will inevitably be debatable.

VIOLENCE

Reading current media, we might think that violence has never been worse. Below are some examples to demonstrate the sorts of violence from 50 years ago that seem barbaric by today's standards:

- The US thought it was acceptable to use napalm, often with civilian casualties.[12] Cluster bombs were okay too — 270 million of them in Laos alone without acknowledging at the time they were even there.[13]
- Soviet tanks rolled through the streets of Prague to keep the population in its place.
- Large parts of current Germany were subject to the repressive Stasi police that was moving on from direct torture to perfect psychological harassment (Zersetzung[14]).
- The British and Irish were engaging in 'The Troubles' which by most measures is vastly worse than terrorism today.
- In Chile, 3000 of Pinochet's opponents

disappeared — almost certainly murdered but probably tortured as well.

- In Spain, it is thought Franco's favoured form of torture for his political opponent was a screw through the back of the neck.[15]

- In most countries, it was legal and accepted for government employees to hit citizens with a stick (teachers hitting students).

This list is from the histories of OECD countries. Whatever we think of our current politicians and state violence, it's got nothing on 50 years ago. I don't think anyone would want to go back to the more violent state of the world back then, so all we can debate is the slope of the line (Figure 30).

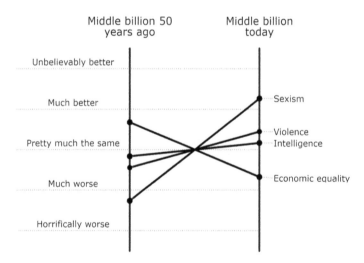

Figure 30 It was undoubtedly more violent 50 years ago. Source: *Comparonomics.com.*

It is hard sometimes to acknowledge that things have got better when they are still unacceptably bad. Nothing about this analysis is an excuse for today's violence. The book *Factfulness* made the point nicely:

> I am saying that things can be both bad and better...I see no conflict between celebrating this progress and continuing to fight for more.

SEXUAL FREEDOM — HOMOPHOBIA

One encouraging trend in the last 50 years is the speed at which we have become accepting of non-heterosexual preferences. Below are a few stories to illustrate how things used to be:

- In most countries, you could be locked up — up to 20 years — for being homosexual.
- Homosexuality was listed in the *Diagnostic and Statistical Manual* (DSM), the bible of psychology, as a pathological illness or mental disorder.
- Words like 'homo', 'faggot' and 'poofter' were not that uncommon and undoubtedly not considered with the same disdain as today.
- It wasn't that long before then that chemical or physical castration was considered an appropriate treatment for homosexuality.[16]
- In the US, even the American Civil Liberties Union wouldn't take on cases to challenge homosexual laws until the 1960s.[17]
- Gay marriage was not even considered a possibility.

It seems astonishing how much attitudes have changed since then. In Ireland where 78% of people identify themselves as Catholic, they elected an openly gay prime minister. There are still plenty of folks who are horrified at the acceptance of this 'immoral' behaviour. I suggest that most of us now don't give a damn about people's sexual preferences and see the correction of this past injustice as a good thing. You can only draw a relatively steep line for this trend (Figure 31).

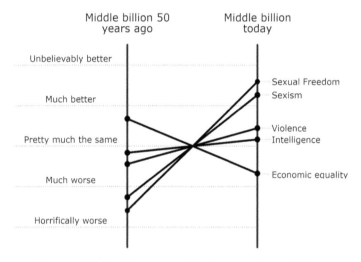

Figure 31 We have become significantly more tolerant of alternative sexual preferences. Source: *Comparonomics.com.*

RACISM

It's clear that issues of racism are far from solved and it's maddening we still need movements like Black Lives Matter, but let's list a few stories from 50 years ago:

- Most countries with high immigration had openly racist immigration policies — Canada, Australia, New Zealand and the US all had strong biases for white immigrants.

- Interracial marriage wasn't legal in all states in the US until 1967.[18] Back then about 20% of people approved of marriage between blacks and whites, now it is 87%.[19]

- In Australia up to the 1970s, the government was forcibly removing 'half-caste' children from Aboriginal mothers, so the children could be better integrated into white society. These children were known as the stolen generation.[20] Aboriginals were not recognised as citizens until 1967 and could not own property in Queensland until 1975.

- In the early 1960s, French police massacred between 200 and 300 unarmed Algerian protesters in the heart of Paris.[21]

- Canada still had a policy of forcibly removing indigenous children from their families and into Christian boarding schools. The goal was to help them assimilate or 'kill the Indian in the child.'[22]

The selection of things listed here seems outrageously racist now, and it's by no means a comprehensive list. The fact that we have become less racist most of us believe is a good thing, and hopefully the improvements will accelerate (Figure 32).

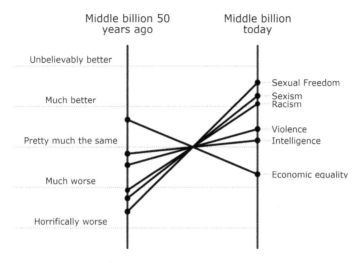

Figure 32 It was a lot more racist 50 years ago.

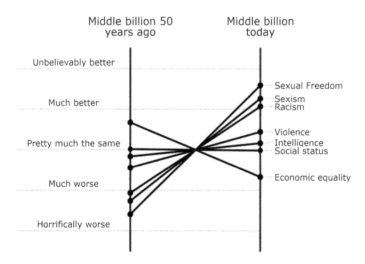

Figure 33 Social status for average people in each time period is obviously the same. Source: Comparonomics.com.

SOCIAL STATUS

Change in social status (Figure 33) is the least debatable because we are comparing average people of one time to average people of another. Social status is the same because it is a relative thing. It also shows that some things don't change and is a contrast to the King Louis example where he had a much higher social status. This is something explored in more detail later.

PERCEPTION OF HAPPINESS

There is a sense that lots of people are struggling, there is a loss of social cohesion, more depression and people seem angrier than they used to be. This particular social change is very personal and quite hard to define due to lack of adequate information from 50 years ago. Where there are long-term studies, they don't conclusively indicate that we are significantly unhappier. However, I'm going to suggest that there is a perception of general grumpiness and at least the perception that lots of us are worse off. This perception of unhappiness is odd given many other economic and social trends seem to be in a positive direction. However, a core part of this investigation is to work out why our perceptions can be so different from reality. The entire second section of this book identifies the reasons we systematically feel gloomy about progress and life.

Appendix 2 also shows how you can use comparonomic graphs to represent a completely different worldview. What if you have a completely different set of social trends that are important to you? Well, you can scribble them down; when you do, it makes it easier to communicate with those who have different views on the world.

SUMMARY OF SOCIAL CHANGES OVER 50 YEARS

The most significant conclusion from this short analysis is that most social trends tend to be in a positive direction. We are less racist, sexist, homophobic, and violent. Maybe society is not falling apart but getting a little more compassionate. Remember that this is not a comprehensive list of socially significant topics, but it does appear from this selection that things are getting better.

One thing from this selection that does seem to have got worse is income inequality, but not by a massive amount. I will discuss this later in the book, but as a spoiler alert, the whole story of this book is not about the doom of increasing inequality.

It is worth reminding you to have a bit of a think about where this book's line of reasoning is leading — what is making us feel so bad given both the economic and social trends are consistently heading in a positive direction?

CHAPTER CONCLUSIONS

We have surveyed several social trends to see how they have changed and to show how comparonomic graphs can be used for non-economic questions. If we are looking out over time, there appears to be an extensive range of social changes that are trending in the direction of treating people more equally instead of judging them based on race, sex, religion, and sexual preference. If there is a trend, it seems that the rate of change is accelerating. For example, it took a long time for women to be given the vote everywhere for the middle billion. It started in New Zealand in 1893, but the Swiss didn't complete it till 1971. The change in perceptions about homosexuality seems to have changed at a much faster rate.

It is easy to forget the progress we have made given the world was almost universally homophobic, sexist, and racist as little as 100 years ago. It is good that we treat small steps backward with such outrage. The banning of people from majority Muslim countries in the US is a good example. It is excellent we are outraged but easy to forget how recently most nations had or still have race or religious based immigration policies.

The comparonomic graph is a simple way to explicitly express your view on how you think this has changed without any hidden assumptions. It is an elegant, simple way to show different values and explicitly how we think things have changed.

These tools could also be used to do a similar analysis for the environment and Appendix 2 has some pointers on that. Hopefully with this perspective of how relatively well we are doing it means we are more likely to place a higher value on protecting the environment.

The critical question asked in Part One of this book is how well are we doing compared to people in the past? The answer is almost universally pretty damn well. The core, more baffling question is if we are doing so well, why don't we feel like we are doing well? I suspect it is not just about convincing people they are doing well — the angst is real and needs investigating, which is what Part Two of the book covers.

PART II
HOW DO WE THINK WE ARE DOING?

6

IF THINGS ARE SO MUCH BETTER, WHY DO WE FEEL SO BAD?

HOPEFULLY, Part One made a strong case that things have never been better in numerous ways. The core idea I want to explore is that given things are so good, why do we feel so bad? *The Economist* has a nice summary of this current dissatisfaction:

> Indeed, for most people on Earth, there has never been a better time to be alive. Large parts of the West, however, do not see it that way. For them, progress happens mainly to other people. Wealth does not spread itself, new technologies destroy jobs that never come back, an underclass is beyond help or redemption, and other cultures pose a threat—sometimes a violent one.[1]

Yuval Noah Harari came to a similar conclusion:

> After centuries of economic growth and scientific progress, life should have become calm and peaceful, at

least in the most advanced countries. If our ancestors knew what tools and resources stand ready at our command, they would have surmised that we must be enjoying celestial tranquility, free of all cares and worries. The truth is very different. Despite all our achievements, we feel a constant pressure to do and produce even more.[2]

The reasons for our dissatisfaction are a mixture of well-known issues like media bias for bad news and less well-known ones like nostalgia bias where things from the past frequently seem better than they were.

We are familiar with the term 'feel-good factors' that make us feel better. This list is the opposite — a list of feel-bad factors. These feel-bad factors all add to each other to make life appear worse than it is. Think of this list as similar to cognitive biases developed by Amos Tversky and Daniel Kahneman,[3] who document systematic flaws in how we think about decisions. Their work highlighted the 'mental fog' that stops people perceiving decisions logically. This work led to the development of behavioural economics which focuses on the quirks in people's actual decision-making. The list developed here attempts to define mental quirks or biases relevant to long-term economic and social development trends.[4]

There has been a considerable amount of research, over numerous years, describing a wide range of cognitive biases. If you are not familiar with the idea of cognitive biases, there is an excellent list in Wikipedia that gives a high-level summary and references for further reading.[5] What I have tried to do in this chapter is to work out which of these biases and social norms form the basis that cause us to look so negatively on human progress.

You may be immune to a few of the biases listed below, but I have tried to include as many as possible that may be an issue for at least some people. Before jumping into the list, it is worth making your own one and then seeing how it compares to what is compiled here. You may well have some biases I have entirely missed. The feel-bad factors are categorised into the following groupings:

- Information-gathering biases — systematic issues with how we receive information.
- Thinking biases — how we think about information that we gather.
- Social expectation bias — how social norms influence our perceptions and behaviour.
- Economic model bias — how economic models influence us even though they may not accurately reflect reality.
- Economic inequality biases — how we see ourselves in relation to others.

These groupings are arbitrary. It would be possible to make inequality as a subset of social expectations or thinking bias, but they are grouped like this as it forms a useful way to view the different types of feel-bad factors.

Each of the feel-bad factors in the following chapters are discussed as briefly as possible with links for more information if you want to follow up. People have written books about most of them, but my goal is to give you a high-level summary of each, so you can get a feel for how many feel-bad factors there are, and how they combine to make us feel worse about progress. What was genuinely surprising was how many feel-bad factors there seem to be.

7

INFORMATION-GATHERING BIASES

THE FOLLOWING feel-bad factors relate to how we obtain information. Some information sources have been with us for many years, and some are new, but it is worth thinking about our sources of information and how they could impact how we think about human progress.

MEDIA — WE HAVE EVOLVED TO SEEK BAD NEWS

Media preference for bad news is a well-documented bias that has a logical evolutionary explanation. As we evolved, there was a natural tendency to pay more attention to negative information. Data that indicates you are about to be eaten or attacked is naturally more significant than everything else. This core evolutionary preference is part of the reason that we are drawn to read bad news.[1] There is evidence that parts of our brain are more alert for negative information, our amygdala is hijacked.[2]

Media know that bad news sells and that is why they deliver it to us. Do you remember the list of catastrophes that were once imminent threats to humanity?

- Population explosion and subsequent famine
- Y2K
- The ozone hole
- Acid rain
- Aids
- SARS
- Ebola
- Nuclear holocaust
- Running out of oil
- Mad cow disease.

The reason for lots of bad news is not necessarily that the world is bad, we are told about the negative stuff more often. Gradual improvement is, by definition, not news. You will never see the headline 'Another 13,000 people escape extreme poverty today'. This has happened every day on average for 20 years and is great news but not newsworthy.[3] The news is inherently biased towards violent events because of the simple fact that they are events. Max Roser, an economist at Oxford University who collects data on the world's development, puts it this way:

> Things that happen in an instant are mostly bad. It's this earthquake or that horrible murder. You're never going to have an article on the BBC or CNN that begins by saying: 'There's no famine in south London today' or:

'Child mortality again decreased by 0.005% in Botswana.'[4]

The American public radio journalist Eric Weiner says, 'the truth is that unhappy people, living in profoundly unhappy places, make for good stories.' There is an excellent detailed summary of the media biases that cause a dim outlook on life in the epilogue of the book *Progress* by Johan Norberg.[5]

Strong media is an essential part of democracy and one of the key reasons we are able to solve many problems in the world but it is inherently negative.

Just because there is a lot of bad news doesn't mean the world is bad.

SOCIAL MEDIA

There are plenty of good things about social media but there is also growing evidence that in many cases it makes us feel worse. Our tendency to feel worse was summed up nicely by Theodore Roosevelt: 'Comparison is the thief of joy.' You are pottering along nicely; then you see what someone else has and naturally want that too. Social media has two main ways it amplifies this problem. First, it is possible to compare yourself to a lot more people. Probably even worse is that people publish polished versions of their lives. There are photos of exotic holidays, the great parties and their success at everything. You can't help but make the comparison and feel a little inadequate. Gore Vidal put it nicely: 'Whenever a friend succeeds, a little something in me dies.' We can now see a constant flow of mini-successes by those close to us that could well add to making us feel bad.

The exact mechanisms for feeling inadequate probably can't be known, but there is growing evidence of the harmful mental impact of social media. Researchers in Denmark split 1095 daily Facebook users into two groups, half given access to the site as usual and the remainder forced to quit cold turkey. They found that after a week, those on a break from the social network felt 55% less stressed.[6] A *Harvard Business Review* article concludes the more you use Facebook, the worse you feel.[7] It would not surprise me if we look back at unregulated social media as the equivalent of information crack cocaine.

To be balanced there is also evidence that social media can be useful for you too. The fact that we spend so much time on it shows that we value the ability to interact with a wide range of people in ways that we never previously could. The fact that the President of USA was banned for inciting violence indicates some real issues with free-for-all social media. The point of the section though is to highlight the potential risks of gathering information from social media and how it can contribute to why we don't feel so good about life and progress.

Most of the other information feel-bad factors on the list have been around for a while but social media is relatively new. Social media may have ramped up our feelings of dissatisfaction despite the reality of life getting better. How we receive information can make a big difference in our perceptions.

Just because we feel bad after spending time on social media doesn't mean life is bad.

PERVASIVE ADVERTISING

The goal of advertising is to make you want something you don't currently have, so you buy the product or service they are pushing. J. Walker Smith, of Yankelovich Partners, in 2004, released his company findings that the average person saw 500 ads per day in the 1960s and 1970s and as of 2004 the average person sees over 5000. The good news here is that some new services like TV on demand and podcasts can dramatically reduce exposure to advertising compared to live TV and radio.

It is hard not to feel a pang of desire on a stormy day when your local travel agent flashes idyllic, sun-drenched images on special just for today. The crispness and size of that flat screen in the window makes my puny TV seem more inadequate each day. There has been much written about social impacts of advertising but rather than dwell on this we'll move on to other less well-known feel-bad factors.

Just because we have a nagging want for more things doesn't mean we are hard done by — it is an inevitable consequence of being surrounded by messages telling us to want more things.

NEGATIVE INFORMATION BIAS

Negative information bias is different from bad news bias, as it is about the way we are more likely to take in any bad news we get from other sources beyond media. There is strong evidence that bad is stronger than good when it comes to information.[8] We have a negativity bias, which is the tendency to give far more attention to negative details than positive ones. Steven Pinker summarised it nicely:

> ... we are more likely to remember losing money, being abandoned by friends or receiving criticism than we are to remember winning money, gaining friends or receiving praise. The authors of a related study point out that negative information receives more processing and contributes more strongly to the final impression than does positive information ... Bad is stronger than good. This is the title of a review article by the psychologist Roy Baumeister in which he reviewed a wide variety of evidence that people are more sensitive to bad things than to good things. If you lose $10, that makes you feel a lot worse than the amount by which you feel better if you gain $10. That is, losses are felt more keenly than gains — as Jimmy Connors once put it, 'I hate to lose more than I like to win.'[9]

My favourite way of describing this bias is by the folk at FutureCrunch,[10] who said negative news is like Velcro on our brains while positive news is like Teflon (you should sign up to their newsletter of good news — it's a brilliant antidote to all the bad news we hear; www.futurecrunch.com). It is typical to remember the bad news but this does not mean that the world is actually bad. It's just the information that sticks most in our minds.

Just because we can recall lots of negative things doesn't mean the world is negative.

DIGITAL SCREEN ADDICTION

Digital screen addiction is possibly a bit of a stretch as to why we don't feel good about things but is included to ensure the list is as broad as possible. There is some evidence that getting information from a digital screen irrespective of what the information is, impacts our mood in a negative way. There is an excellent summary of research showing:

> The more time teens spend looking at screens, the more likely they are to report symptoms of depression.[11]

After frequent use of a smartphone, more people feel lonely.[12] It could well be that it is because of bad news or social media but it could be related to the constant flow of information that we never used to have. It could be related to the constant interruptions in whatever else we are doing rather than the screen itself. Sometimes a picture is worth a thousand words and this Banksy image (Figure 34) nicely captures this new potential feel-bad factor. It doesn't matter what type of information the couple is looking at, it seems unlikely to make them happy.

This feel-bad factor is different than social media or preference for bad news or advertising. It is about how we feel when getting information from screens. It is not clear how important this feel-bad factor is. The mechanism for dissatisfaction could be because we get no relief from a constant flow of information or it could be something related to the screen itself.

Figure 34 Banksy image shows an example of 'sub-optimal' use of screens. Source: PA Images / Alamy Stock Photo.

Just because we feel a constant pull of screens and dissatisfaction from these interactions doesn't necessarily mean the world is a bad place.

SUMMARY OF INFORMATION BIASES

The purpose of this chapter is to think about how we receive information and how that can impact our view of the world. We know that how we collect information from media and advertising can have negative impacts. There is also more knowledge on the way that social media and the constant flow of information from digital screens can affect our outlook on life. These different ways of gathering information illustrate a set of systematic feel-bad factors that make us feel less positive about the world:

- *Just because there is a lot of bad news doesn't mean the world is bad.*
- *Just because we feel bad after spending time on social media doesn't mean life is bad.*
- *Just because we have a nagging want for more things doesn't mean we are hard done by — it is an inevitable consequence of being surrounded by messages telling you to want more things.*
- *Just because we can recall lots of negative things doesn't mean the world is negative.*
- *Just because we feel a constant pull of screens and dissatisfaction from these interactions doesn't necessarily mean the world is a bad place.*

8
THINKING BIASES

This set of biases is separate from how we gather information. They analyse how we think about the information we get. The thinking biases chosen here are not about how we make day-to-day decisions but about how we think about the progress of society.

WE HAVE TIME TO THINK

There is an old saying that when you are hungry, you have one problem. When you have food, you have lots of problems. This line of thinking was highlighted in the book *Homo Deus* by Yuval Noah Harari.

> We have managed to bring famine, plague, and war under
> control thanks largely to our phenomenal economic
> growth, which provides us with abundant food, medicine,
> energy and raw materials.[1]

For most of human history we have been working on keeping famine, plague, or war at bay. Now they are mostly sorted (significant nasty blip for Covid, of course), we have a whole range of new 'high quality' problems. The comparonomic graphs allow you to systematically see the dramatic progress we have been making. Many of the issues even our parents had, we no longer have. A good way to think about whatever issues are on your mind is to consider how nice it is to have time to think about them. Almost certainly your ancestors didn't have time to think about such relatively trivial things.

I remember watching two siblings debating vigorously (this is a kind way to describe it) the pros and cons of different hair conditioners with their parent at the store. This was a real problem for them, but with a little perspective, not so much. I'm sure you have many of the same stories where people get upset about the most mundane things. I can be guilty of this and it can feel genuine at the time, but it doesn't mean the world is turning to custard.

Just because you have time to think about problems doesn't mean they are important problems on the scale of things.

NOSTALGIA BIAS — WHY THE PAST FEELS SO GOOD

Nothing is more responsible for the good old days than a bad memory.[2]

Nostalgia is not a new thing. There are references to it going back to the English peasant revolt of 1381 talking about the past golden age of a nostalgic image of rural bliss.[3] A medieval proverb states 'It is the evening that we look back on the day with pleasure.' Medieval literature is littered with references to the good old days. The Chaucer poem *The Former Age* has the lines:

> *a blissful, peaceful and sweet life*
> *was led by people in the olden days.*

The term 'nostalgia' was invented by Johannes Hofer as a Swiss doctor in 1688 when observing levels of homesickness of mercenary soldiers. Originally it described a longing for home; now it is a longing for the past. In 1777 David Hume noted that:

> the humor of blaming the present, and admiring the past,
> is strongly rooted in human nature.

The formal name for the cognitive bias where people tend to view the past favourably is called 'rosy retrospection'.[4] This may have some personal benefits in that it helps people's self-esteem[5] and sense of well-being, but it does not accurately help understand how the world has progressed and what we might do to make it better in the future. Steven Pinker summarised this nostalgia perception nicely:

> People always pine for a golden age. They're nostalgic about an era in which life was simpler and more predictable. The psychologist, Roger Eibach, has argued that this is because people confuse changes in themselves with changes in the times. As we get older, certain things

inevitably happen to us. We take on more responsibilities, so we have a greater cognitive burden. We become more vigilant about threats, especially as we become parents.[6]

Nostalgia bias is a cognitive flaw that has been the backbone of significant political changes recently. We now have politics of nostalgia rather than politics of progress, e.g. Make America Great Again. The assumption that the old days were better is possibly at the core of Brexit as well.[7] Having a misconception about the past can have significant consequences on current political choices: it is not an academic nicety to understand these things but has significant real-world consequences.

If you step through the questions in previous chapters to think about how things have changed, then talking about the good old days often means we were poorer, more homophobic, violent, sexist, and racist. While some people may actively want to choose a society like that, I doubt this is what most would choose, so being aware of nostalgia bias is essential.

For most countries that make up the middle billion, the population is aging. This means a more substantial proportion of people that are looking back on the 'good old days'. This aging could be making the nostalgia bias more prominent than it used to be. It is hard to know if this demographic change is significant, but it is included here as another point that could be worth considering.

Just because it feels like they were good old days doesn't mean they were actually better.

HEADWINDS/TAILWINDS ASYMMETRY

A fascinating piece of research by Tom Gilovich and Shai Davidai has identified that people naturally think about things that make their lives harder rather than easier.[8] This bias gets its name from the observation that when biking we notice the headwind but quickly forget the tailwind. Their clever analysis shows that people think their siblings had it easier, their sports teams have harder draws, other academics have it easier, and 'the system' is stacked against their political party.

The most straightforward example is that they would ask siblings which one had it easiest and universally people seemed to think that their siblings had it easier. This undoubtedly can't be true and, because they have shown it over a range of topics, it seems to be a verifiable psychological basis. It is normal to feel hard done by, even when you are not.

The other bit of their research showed that getting people to think about whether they have it easy or hard forces people into more questionable ethical behaviour. If people believe that things are much harder for them than others, they seem to be prepared to push ethical boundaries to make up for their 'disadvantage'. This seemingly natural feeling of being disadvantaged leads to resentfulness and as Gilovich and Davidai point out, 'resentment — doesn't make us our best selves.'

One of the goals of this book is to create tools that allow you to ask questions so you can prove to yourself that you have a lot to be grateful for. The fact that you didn't necessarily feel grateful before is very typical but doesn't make it right. For whatever reason, our brain plays a trick on us, thinking we are hard done by when in fact we are not. The headwind/tailwind asymmetry is something worth being aware of.

Just because you feel hard done by doesn't mean you are actually hard done by.

CONFIRMATION BIAS

Confirmation bias is potentially one of the most potent sources of distortions of our judgments. We seek out evidence to support what we already believe. Like everyone else, I place more value on evidence that supports my own biases. I love a 'wine is good for you' story and skip over the 'alcohol causes your bits to fall off' stories. Maybe the confirmation bias has driven the creation of this book. For whatever reason, I've long been fascinated with how much progress we make but how much we grumble about things. I've crafted a tool to make it easy for folks to gauge for themselves how things have changed. I was, however, surprised how easy it is to show how wrong the standard economic models are at gauging progress and how many genuine feel-bad factors there are that conspire to make us gloomier. Economists are acutely aware how susceptible we are to confirmation bias.

Few enjoy the feeling of being caught out in an error. But real trouble starts when the desire to avoid a reckoning leads to a refusal to grapple with contrary evidence. Economists often assume that people are rational. Faced with a new fact, rational actors should update their view of the world in order to take better decisions in future. Yet years of economic research illuminate the ways in which human cognition veers from rationality. Studies confirm what is obvious from experience: people frequently disregard information that conflicts with their view of the world.[9]

Confirmation bias is a meta-bias. If you are particularly susceptible to this one, then your ability to learn from new information is severely limited. Consider the list of things below and whether you have held the same view your whole life. It doesn't matter what the view is, just how long you have had it:

- Always voted for the same political party or never read a policy from the other side.
- Never got more or less religious or never changed your religion.
- Always had the same view on the Palestinians and Israelis (one is the victim and the other the criminal or the other way around).
- Always had the same view on the state and risks of global warming (whether it is or isn't an issue).
- Always supported the same sports team — still watch the same sport.
- Always lived in the same place and thought it the best place ever.

- You have the same thoughts your whole life on vegetarianism.
- Your opinion on both male and female circumcision cuts one way only.

If you have changed your mind on all these things all the time, then maybe you are a bit unstable but, if you have never changed your mind on any of them, then one of two options is possible:

- Your combination of beliefs on a wide range of controversial things from years ago is right and always has been — pretty unlikely, don't you think?
- You are susceptible to confirmation bias and only take information that supports your current view on things.

I suspect folks picking up this book are aware of, and on the lookout for, confirmation bias. If you had levels of scepticism about the trends in Chapter 4 on progress over the last 50 years because they did not fit your gut views, it is worth redoing that analysis when you are aware of all the perfectly reasonable feel-bad factors listed in this chapter.

Confirmation bias tends to suck people into opposing trenches that reinforce battles. This is captured beautifully in a chart produced by the *Economist* that shows the books people read on Amazon are from their own bubble view of the world.[10] I'd suggest it is braver to jump out of the trench and have a cup of tea in the middle.

This confirmation bias is probably more of a risk in larger countries like the US where the population is large enough to support media channels with entirely different views of the world.

While confirmation bias is not inherently harmful, when combined with all the other feel-bad factors, it can reinforce the view that the world is not progressing very well.

Just because you find lots of information to support your views doesn't mean your views are infallible — you could probably find lots of information that would support alternative opinions, but you tend not to.

AVAILABILITY HEURISTIC

At its simplest, the availability heuristic[11] or bias means we remember stories about things we have recently heard more than data. What is more convincing and memorable: the fact that women couldn't vote in Switzerland and forms of rape were legal in the US in 1970, or some data on the rate of increase of women's workforce participation? The availability heuristic feel-bad factor is tightly linked to confirmation bias as we seek stories to confirm our views and negativity bias that means bad news sticks more than good news.

The availability heuristic is not inherently negative though. This book purposefully uses memorable stories as opposed to reams of data in the previous chapters to provide evidence for things getting better, so it is not always a feel-bad factor. It is, however, worth being aware that a story of a lone attacker with a knife somewhere near to you is not proof of an increase in violence even though it feels like it. Or a hard-luck story of a family fallen on tough times is not proof that the economy is screwed.

Just because you remember some stories that stick in your head doesn't necessarily prove anything about overall trends.[12]

PESSIMISM BIAS

The pessimism bias is defined as 'the tendency for some people to overestimate the likelihood of negative things happening to them.' It is closely related to the negativity bias where we tend to remember negative things. When you project forward, you will assume that bad things will happen. Pessimism is historically prevalent, even in the days of Adam Smith:

> Pessimists have always been ubiquitous and have always been feted. Five years have seldom passed away in which some book or pamphlet has not been published, pretending to demonstrate that the wealth of the nation was fast declining, that the country was depopulated, agriculture neglected, manufactures decaying, and trade undone.

Matt Ridley noted:

> A fresh crop of pessimists springs up each decade, unabashed in its certainty that it stands balanced upon

the fulcrum of history ... Doom after doom was promised: nuclear war, pollution, overpopulation, famine, disease, violence, grey goo, vengeful technology — culminating in the eruption of civil chaos that would undoubtedly follow the inability of computers.[13]

If you happen to believe the world is about to collapse due to any number of things from the pending environmental collapse, World War Three, social anarchy, or artificial intelligence servitude, then there is not much anyone can do to help you. By all means do what you can to stop the impending doom but it seems a tenuous argument to assume all the progress to date has been useless due to some unknowable pending future event.[14]

Blind pessimism of inevitable doom is just as extreme as blind optimism that assumes everything will be okay. A constructive middle ground seems more useful but the point of this discussion is to highlight pessimism bias is a very real thing that makes people feel gloomy. I like the conclusion on the balance of these things by Hans Rosling:[15]

> I'm not an optimist. That makes me sound naïve. I'm a very serious 'possibilist.' That's something I made up. It means someone who neither hopes without reason, nor fears without reason, someone who constantly resists the overdramatic worldview. As a possibilist, I see all this progress, and it fills me with conviction and hope that further progress is possible.

Pessimism bias can also manifest itself in a form of irrational fear of things that are relatively low risk. Dan Gardner's book *The Science of Fear*[16] highlights how fear can cause more harm than the actual risks people are afraid of.

> We are the healthiest, wealthiest, and longest-lived people in history. And we are increasingly afraid. This is one of the great paradoxes of our time.

There is a phenomenon related to pessimism bias called the optimism gap. People mostly seem to think their local neighbourhood is safe and their friends are doing okay, but the rest of society is in deep trouble. Your view immediately around you is relatively rosy but for wider society, it is much worse.

In some ways, this pessimism bias is out of the scope of our discussion because I am purposefully trying not to look into the future. It is included here to give an understanding of why so many people may be gloomy and could be a logical conclusion of the other cumulative feel-bad factors. Pessimism bias is a very typical thinking bias but not necessarily accurate.

Just because you feel despondent about the future doesn't mean the future will actually turn out badly.

SUMMARY OF THINKING BIASES

Several thinking biases that have been described by researchers over the years make us believe progress is worse than it really is. What was surprising is how many feel-bad thinking biases there are that seem to make us feel worse about life and progress:

- *Just because you have time to think about problems doesn't mean they are important problems on the scale of things.*
- *Just because it feels like they were good old days doesn't mean they were actually better.*
- *Just because you feel hard done by doesn't mean you are actually hard done by.*
- *Just because you find lots of information to support your views doesn't mean your views are infallible — you could probably find lots of information that would support alternative opinions, but you tend not to.*
- *Just because you remember some stories that stick in your head doesn't necessarily prove anything about overall trends.*
- *Just because you feel despondent about the future doesn't mean the future will actually turn out badly.*

9

SOCIAL EXPECTATION BIASES

THE SOCIAL EXPECTATION set of feel-bad factors are not about how we receive information or about how we think about it, but how social expectations shape how we behave. I'm acutely aware that some of these social expectations are not universal to all of the middle billion but are more quirks of my particular cultural settings. I have put them in not because they are necessarily universal but to illustrate social expectations can have a significant impact on how we think about progress. You may be able to think of others more relevant to your culture.

NATURAL LEVEL OF GRUMPINESS (NLG)

Independent of how good life is, there seems to be a social preference for having a bit of a grumble. Imagine someone has a story about the horrific customer service from a phone or utility company. It's hard not to chip in your own account on the unbelievably lousy service and incompetence from company X when you were trying to do Y — you've got one in your head right now, I'm sure. When these stories pop up, try replying with something like this: 'I haven't had any problems lately — most services are great, and the people I talk to are jolly lovely people.' It is weirdly anti-social not to mostly grumble about how useless things are. I'm no saint — I have my useless customer service stories I love to tell, but it doesn't make it any less odd when you stand back and look at why it is socially acceptable to do this. Why do we so instantly think of things to grumble about rather than the positive stories? It is probably closely related to our preference for bad news, but it is slightly different as it is about what is socially acceptable to discuss. It may be that we are trying to help people by warning them of dangers, or Steven Pinker explains the reason could also be related to social cohesion:

> Another emotional bias is the psychology of moralization. Complaining about problems is a way of sending a signal to others that you care about them, so critics are seen as more morally engaged.[1]

I once sat across from two people having a hard-core grumble about the difficulty of getting a berth for their superyachts at peak times at their favourite tropical island. I was able to confide in them that this has never been a problem for me. Who thought there would be advantages to not owning a superyacht? While it is easy to dismiss the level of angst they felt about this 'problem', it seemed real to them. As discussed previously, we would count this as a 'First World problem' but what we are digging into here is the social expectations around publicly grumbling about stuff.

This natural level of grumpiness becomes apparent when you visit smaller countries, regions or towns. The types of things that people grumble about tend to get more and more minor, not that you would want to point that out given the levels of concern they seem to cause. I read a letter to the editor in a small newspaper that got people fired up because someone counted their refuse bags and got only 49 instead of 52 (one per week). This caused a flurry of other people to check and the local municipality set up a freephone line for people to be able to get their extra bags. And I thought, oh, how lovely that they grumble about such minor things.

You can gauge how well folks are doing by what they grumble about. While the Covid pandemic raged in the rest of the world, the little town in New Zealand I live in that had yet to have a single case was getting grumpy about the pros and cons of putting fairy lights on historic buildings — yes, life is great here ...

As life gets better and better, I suspect we will continue to grumble about things that are genuinely 'First World problems' compared to folks in the past. This is different from having time to think about problems or our preference for bad news and more about the social acceptance of grumbling irrespective of how good life is.

Just because people grumble a lot of the time doesn't mean life is horrible.

POSITIVITY IS UNPOPULAR

I have noticed that when you point out how good life is, it often seems to be wildly unpopular. This is subtly different than preferring to grumble because it is the active aversion to having it pointed out how good things are. John Stuart Mill summed it up nicely in his speech on 'perfectibility':

> I have observed that not the man who hopes when others despair, but the man who despairs when others hope, is admired by a large class of persons as a sage.

A thought-provoking example I had recently was when an acquaintance mentioned they were not keen to travel in Europe due to terrorism threats. I tried to help by showing them a graph of the fall in terrorism deaths in Europe since the 1970s,[2] and they were horrified I believed such a thing. I was trying to be helpful to give them the confidence to enjoy a trip around Europe. However, the consensus of the group discussion seemed to be that it must be fake data and they knew a lot about the threats from Jihadists roaming the streets in Europe (media bad news bias and availability heuristic). I suspect they also know about Europe's past terrorism. It is easy to forget the thousands that died from 'The Troubles' in Ireland and the UK, Basque separatists, hijackings and Lockerbie. It is possible that people don't like their views challenged (confirmation bias), but I've included it as a separate category for feel-bad factors as I'm surprised how often people seemed to think it inappropriate to point out a more positive view on life even when based on uncontested facts.

Another example is that older adults talk about the good old days and, if you point out how racist, sexist, homophobic, unhealthy, and poor it was back then, the confirmation bias kicks in and the hackles go up. I have tried numerous versions of this conversation and I find it odd how socially unacceptable it seems to be to have this conversation. How dare I disturb this evidently incorrect view of history? So, it's not about the social acceptability of grumbling but the social unacceptability of pointing out how good things are these days. Yes, it is probably nostalgia bias, mixed with confirmation bias along with a few others but I thought I'd include it as a separate feel-bad factor. It seems like something different that could stop more correct views of progress propagating through society.

This social dislike of sharing good news about the world is not a good sign for sales of this book — oh well, I've quite enjoyed writing it anyway.

Just because you don't hear many positive stories via your social groups doesn't mean there aren't any — maybe it is socially unacceptable to spread good news.

CULTURAL EXPECTATIONS OF HAPPINESS

In some cultures, particularly in the West, it is expected that you should be happy.[3] However, no matter how good life is overall, the reality is that everyone has ups and downs. If there is an expectation of happiness and you are not happy, then it may well be easy to blame this on the dreadful state of the world. No matter how much progress we make, it seems that we are hardwired to have a bit of joy and a bit of sorrow — it's what makes us human.

Without acknowledging the inevitability of fluctuations in our state of happiness, then the conclusions from this book have the possibility of making people even unhappier. You have now been made aware that you are in the historic 1% most fortunate people to have ever lived. If you know that and you're still unhappy, what a loser you must be ... well, no ... you're just experiencing the inevitable ripples of life.

It is indeed easier to blame something else as to why you feel unhappy, but this becomes a problem if you try to fix 'the world' when it's progressing quite nicely. Even the wealthiest, most fortunate people in the world still have off days. That will always be part of life, and we can't necessarily link it to any general lack of progress of society.

There seems to be an age-related relationship to happiness. You tend to be happiest when you are young or old and grumpiest when around 45–50.[4] This appears to be accurate in a range of cultures and there doesn't seem to be a clear reason why this is the case. With the change in demographics around the world, maybe the average age is moving closer to the bottom of the unhappiness curve? Perhaps this is a cause of society feeling less happy with our progress. This is not likely to be the most significant reason for our collective gloominess, but it is included to tease out an exhaustive list of reasons we may not feel that great about progress.

Not being happy sometimes is part of life and not necessarily related to progress in the world. Unless you are aware of this, you could blame your unhappiness on the state of the world.

Just because you are unhappy doesn't mean the world is falling to pieces.

NEED FOR SOCIAL STATUS

The desire for social status seems like part of nature which is reflected in the social structures of many animal species as well as most cultures. Some people are on top and others are at the bottom, and that is the natural order of social structures. A key reason for not feeling that great is that while we may be better off than people in the past, you may not be better off than people you live with now, and that's what matters. It's not much fun having low social status.

The desire for social status is different from inequality, which I define as purely economic and discuss separately later. Let us imagine a scenario where you created a society where everyone has the same income. I don't think there is anyone who thinks this is possible or even desirable but let's suppose it happened. There may still be a game of social status related to who is the better looking, a better singer, or writer of insightful tweets (there have been some, apparently). With the feel-bad filters like social media, it could amplify feelings of inadequacy about social status.

Social scientists tell a story about a peasant called Vladimir. One day God comes down to him and says: 'I will give you one wish. You can name anything you want, and I will grant it to you.' Vladimir starts to celebrate, but then God lays down a condition. 'Whatever you choose,' He says, 'I will give to your neighbor twice over.' Vladimir frowns and thinks. And then he clicks his fingers. 'I have it,' he says. 'Lord, please take out one of my eyes!' In a sense, Vladimir was blind all along. Fixated by status, he could not bear to see his neighbor do better than him, even if he had to suffer to prevent it.[5]

The visceral need to do better than your neighbour is probably rooted in the biological need to out-compete and survive to pass on your genes. Given we are all likely to survive, we probably need to shake off this need to out-compete the neighbours. I guess we are still competing for mates to pass on our genes so need to puff out our chests and show how great we are. Maybe as we get older and less able to pass on genes, this could be a cause of our mellowing out a little?

The main problem with social status is that it is a zero-sum game. For whatever measure of social status, there will be some high status and some low status. Any level of economic and social progress won't change the fact that some folk are deemed higher status and others lower. There is no way for everyone to win this unless you reject the social status game altogether.

Just because you don't have high social status doesn't mean you have failed and the world is doomed. An inadequate feeling about social status is the inevitable state for most people in a zero-sum social status game.

SUMMARY OF SOCIAL EXPECTATION BIASES

Independent of how we gather information and think about it, there seem to be some social norms or expectations that make it harder to be positive about progress in the world. It seems normal that we grumble about things and it's inappropriate to point out how good life is. Our expectations of happiness and the impossible-to-win game of social status also seem likely to make us feel worse about the real state of the world.

- *Just because people grumble a lot of the time doesn't mean life is horrible.*
- *Just because you don't hear many positive stories via your social groups doesn't mean there are not any — maybe it is socially unacceptable to spread good news.*
- *Just because you are unhappy doesn't mean the world is falling to pieces.*
- *Just because you don't have high social status doesn't mean you have failed and the world is doomed. An inadequate feeling about social status is the inevitable state for most people in a zero-sum social status game.*

10

ECONOMIC MODEL BIASES

THIS CATEGORY of feel-bad factors relates not to how well we are doing but to how well economists tell us we are doing. Now, you may not care what they say, but it seems that output from the models these economists use have an impact on the mood of society. 'The economy is booming' elicits a different response to 'The economy is in a severe recession.' Being told you are doing no better than folks 50 years ago rankles and makes you think things are not right.

CONVENTIONAL ECONOMIC MODELS ARE WRONG

I struggled with saying economic models are wrong given I believe the saying that 'all models are wrong, but some are useful.' Calling this section something more accurately like 'Conventional economic models are sub-optimal' didn't do justice to how inappropriate some economic models are. The King Louis example was created to demonstrate how useless these models can be. Not all economic models of the past are this bad but enough are, and they seem to impact social sentiment. These models and associated feelings need to be called out for their inaccuracy.

As discussed earlier, there is a strong narrative that suggests the middle billion are no better off than 50 years ago when the previous chapters indicate we are vastly better off. It is easy to dismiss the analysis of economists but their conclusions make it into mainstream thinking. It is not unusual to see the following type of statements written as fact:

> For the first time in more than 100 years the current generation of workers — millennials — are doing worse than the generation before them. — *Business Insider*[1]

> For most workers, real wages have barely budged for decades. — Pew Research[2]

> Since the early 1970s, the hourly inflation-adjusted wages received by the typical worker have barely risen, growing only 0.2% per year. — *Harvard Business Review*[3]

> Millennials are worse off than their parents. — *Financial Times*[4]

> A combination of stagnant living standards for the broad middle of society and an accumulation of unusable extra wealth by the rich has pushed fairness to the top of public argument. – *The Economist*[5]

Let us pause for a moment and consider the likelihood that all these analyses are, shall we say, sub-optimal. It seems way more likely that the analysis in this book is wrong and all the experts are right, surely? The whole point of the first analysis of King Louis was to show how inadequate this type of 'real dollar' analysis is when the goods and services change dramatically. For the comparison from 50 years ago you can make your own analysis and show for almost everything, we wouldn't swap the goods and services the middle billion had then for what we have now. Yet some economic models tell us we are no better off.

What I'm arguing here is that one of the reasons we feel so bad about progress is that many experts tell us we are not doing very well, and they are wrong. Now, don't expect all the experts to come out and say 'Duh — didn't think about that. What we've been doing for fifty years is not right — sorry about that.' It's not the way changes in understanding happen in any field. It is worth considering how important it would be if they are incorrect and, in fact, we are doing rather well.

I have tried hard not to be another expert telling you how things are but to give you the tools to work it out yourself. The list of feel-bad factors in this section is about explaining all the quirks that create real feelings that seem to support the incorrect idea that progress has stalled or is going backward.

How much damage has an inaccurate view of economic progress inflicted on society? Imagine for a moment if we did agree the new form of economic growth measurement was more accurate and, in fact, the economy was growing faster than ever in the history of the world. Would it change how we perceive things and what we prioritise? I suspect so. Our analysis shows that the speed at which goods and services are making their way from impossible to available to everyone has never been faster — how cool is that? Surely that is a better way to think about progress.

Just because economists tell us we are no better off doesn't mean it's true.

NAGGING NEED FOR PROGRESS

As a species, we have been in abject poverty for 99% of our existence and by all comparisons we are now knocking it out of the park. That nagging need for progress may be what has helped drag us out of the caves but is the continued desperate need for improvement still worth the anguish it causes?

This constant need to make more progress is an embedded part of the economic system that we accept blindly, and wanting to go faster gives us a continual sense of not being good enough. The fact we never run fast enough makes for a sense of inadequacy that is insatiable. This is a constant economic feel-bad factor.

I'm not immune from this nagging need for progress. After finishing a project at home, I wander around admiring it for about a week before plotting the next plan and wishing it could get done faster. A great result at work that makes me jump for joy at the time is quickly replaced by the next thing on the list I must get done.

While many of the things that make our lives miraculous creep up slowly, like improvements in medicine, sometimes things progress from impossible to indispensable in the blink of an eye. I love the story told by Louis CK[6] about getting on a flight across the US when Wi-Fi first became available:

> 'I was on an airplane, and there was high-speed Internet on the airplane. That's the newest thing that I know exists. And I'm sitting on the plane, and they go, open up your laptop, you can go on the Internet.
>
> 'And it's fast, and I'm watching YouTube clips. It's amazing—I'm on an airplane! And then it breaks down. And they apologize, the Internet's not working. And the guy next to me goes, "This is bullshit!" I mean, how quickly does the world owe him something that he knew existed only ten seconds ago?'

The technologies behind all those packets of data to make Wi-Fi work are astounding, let alone the fact you are flying in a tin can at 900 km/hour, part of an industry that landed nearly 40 million flights in a year without a single fatal accident![7] I find it amazing that a machine as complex as an airplane operated by creatures as quirky as humans could do that many flights without a crash — unbelievable.

This nagging need for progress seems to be as much an issue for even the super-wealthy as us regular folks. I remember reading about a wealthy person with a love for unique travel experiences way off the beaten path. The person tasked with curating these once-in-a-lifetime experiences would inevitably be quizzed in detail before the end of the current experience about the next day's adventure. Yeah, this is good but what's next?

On finally reaching a lifelong goal of becoming a billionaire, you realise you are at the bottom of the list of billionaires. What a loser. You need to be at least in the top half of the billionaire list. There is no end.

The best discussion I've seen on how to alleviate this nagging need to get more done and have more is the book *Four Thousand Weeks* by Oliver Burkeman. The secret is not more to-do lists but to take a chill pill and realise life is short. There is no way to do everything you want to do, so just focus on a few things and enjoy.

The need for progress is not related to an absolute amount of economic output but a need for a continual increase not just for an individual but for the whole community. An example of this is a recession. Imagine the awful outcome of five years of reduction in GDP by, say, 2% per year. We would all be miserable — five years of recession. But if you compare it to how life was back three to four years previously, the GDP was the same, but there was no perception of misery. Was it miserable a few years ago because GDP was lower?[8] No, what makes a recession miserable is not making progress. We have this trained expectation not for a given level of wealth but to know that it will keep increasing. We have a total aversion to the idea of ever going backward.

The nagging need for progress is not necessarily bad. It may be what has pushed development so far and so fast and the reason for many amazing modern things. It is worth knowing that this need can never be satisfied by getting things done. This constant need for more is the cause of the feeling of helplessness for some, and resetting expectations may help better manage this feel-bad feeling.

Just because we feel the need to make more economic progress and don't make as much as we may like, it doesn't mean our progress so far is hopeless.

SUMMARY OF ECONOMIC MODEL BIASES

I put the economic model biases in a separate chapter because they are different from information-gathering, thinking, and social expectation biases. What if the experts are wrong and instead of struggling we are actually doing okay? What if we can never satisfy our nagging need for more?

- *Just because economists tell us we are no better off, it doesn't mean it's true.*
- *Just because we feel the need to make more economic progress and don't make as much as we may like, it doesn't mean our progress so far is hopeless.*

11

ECONOMIC INEQUALITY BIASES

ECONOMIC INEQUALITY IS its own section of feel-bad factors because they are quite different from information, thinking, economic, or social biases. It is worth considering three entirely different aspects of inequality. First, there is the feeling injustice inequality elicits, which is somewhat different from how it impacts peoples' ability to participate in the economy. Perceptions on why people end up at a different level on the economic hierarchy also create different views on progress.

INEQUALITY — SEEMS SO UNFAIR

There is a famous experiment with monkeys that shows the primal feeling of unfairness caused by inequality.[1] Both monkeys are given cucumbers, and both are happy. Suddenly, one of the monkeys is given grapes while the other still receives cucumber. The cucumber-receiving monkey becomes visibly upset and throws their cucumber at the researcher. It doesn't seem fair that others have something better. We all know the feeling and it seems common throughout the animal kingdom. People also seem to be egalitarian by nature, and unequal societies tend to have an undercurrent of resentment and dissatisfaction.

Part One of this book shows that from a historic point of view, today's middle billion are in the 1% richest to have ever lived. As Yuval Noah Harari[2] eloquently points out, this may not count for much:

> People usually compare themselves to their more fortunate contemporaries rather than to their ill-fated ancestors. If you tell a poor American in a Detroit slum that he has access to much better healthcare than his great-grandparents did a century ago, it is unlikely to cheer him up. Indeed, such talk will sound terribly smug and condescending. 'Why should I compare myself to nineteenth-century factory workers or peasants?' he would retort. 'I want to live like the rich people on television, or at least like the folks in the affluent suburbs.'

Thomas Piketty[3] has raised the awareness and understanding of how the structure of our economy may naturally cause this inequality to continue to rise. This is an issue given how we naturally feel about the unfairness of inequality. However, this increasing inequality and the real associated feelings of injustice does not mean that we are not making progress overall.

Just because others have more than you and it feels unfair, it doesn't mean you are not much better off than you used to be.

PEOPLE CAN'T PARTICIPATE DUE TO INEQUALITY

Beyond the perceived unfairness of inequality is the real crippling inability of those with less to be able to participate with the rest of society.

Being poor is something maybe everyone should experience at some stage. At least when I was poor, I knew it was probably temporary so I didn't feel there was no escape. I went for several years without a social life because I couldn't afford the typical things expected. The sports activities weren't prohibitively expensive but the expectation to take your turn shouting a round of drinks was not in my budget — so I couldn't participate. It sucked. This is not a perception thing but levels of inequality determine who can participate in different activities in society. It is the only feel-bad factor that is not a perception thing but a real barrier to what you can and can't do. Participating in the community is probably a core social need that inequality puts real barriers around.

The barriers to participation caused by inequality, as much as they suck, are not new and have on the scale of things probably only got a little worse relative to the massive progress the bulk of us have been making over time. I'm not saying we shouldn't address it, but it is probably only part of the reason we don't feel so good about progress.

Just because you can't participate in everything you would like to doesn't mean we are not making progress overall.

BELIEF IN MERITOCRACY

The definition of meritocracy is 'a social system, society, or organization in which people have power and success because of their abilities, not because of their money or social position or luck.' If you compare it to an inherited class system, the people at the top know they got there by the chance of being born into the right family. In a meritocracy, they think they are top dog because they deserve it and are better, rather than luckier, than other folk. Even worse is the loss of dignity for those on the bottom rungs of the economy. In the inherited class system, they certainly feel unlucky and that it's not fair. If you believe in meritocracy, it is more socially brutal. I'm at the bottom because I deserve to be there, not because I'm unlucky but because I'm useless. If you believe in meritocracy, it could make inequality feel even worse. Alain de Botton summarised it nicely in his book *Status Anxiety*[4]:

> Low status came to seem not merely regrettable, but also deserved ... To the injury of poverty, a meritocratic system now added the insult of shame.

There is, however, an extensive range of evidence that luck, money, and social position play a much more significant role in where we end up economically.[5] Sure, you need hard work and to have talent but you also get lucky — or unlucky. Robert H. Frank has beautifully articulated these ideas in his book *Success and Luck: Good Fortune and the Myth of Meritocracy*.[6] Most people when they stop and think about it can recall the good luck that has made it possible for them to be successful. Some people don't think they had any luck but they are, let's say, a special breed. If you don't believe in luck and only believe in meritocracy and you're at the bottom of the pile, then you will inevitably feel worse about your place in life. This is another different feel-bad factor that makes you feel worse about the world.

As you can tell from the discussion, I tend not to think the outcome is based purely on skill. Bill Gates and Mark Zuckerberg are unlikely to have done so well if born in Belarus. Where they were born was lucky, plus many other things along the way that they openly acknowledge. However, if we believe it is all about skill but that is not the case, then this seems likely to make us feel a tad unsatisfied.

Your outcome in life will most likely be a mixture of luck, skill, and effort but the point of this section is to show evidence that luck still plays a significant role. Most importantly, if you are told it is all skill and effort yet chance is a crucial part and you end up at the bottom, this seems a particularly cruel outcome. It also means that those that have done well need to keep an eye on their humbleness.

Just because you are wildly successful economically doesn't necessarily mean you are better than anyone else. Just because you are not so successful doesn't necessarily mean you are any worse than other folks.

SUMMARY OF ECONOMIC INEQUALITY BIASES

I have highlighted three entirely different aspects of the concept of inequality that causes us to feel worse about progress. There is the core injustice that appears to be a natural part of human psyche. Inequality also puts real boundaries on your ability to participate in society. Whether you think inequality is due to luck or skill also can amplify the feelings of inadequacy or superiority.

- *Just because others have more than you and it feels unfair doesn't mean you are not much better off than you used to be.*
- *Just because you can't participate in everything you would like to doesn't mean we are not making progress.*
- *Just because you are wildly successful economically doesn't necessarily mean you are better than anyone else.*
- *Just because you are not so successful doesn't necessarily mean you are any worse than other folks.*

12

SUMMARY AND DISCUSSION OF FEEL-BAD FACTORS

THE PREVIOUS CHAPTERS have identified and discussed 20 different 'feel-bad factors' that make us feel worse about the current state of the world. When I started the list years ago, there were four or five, and it has grown as I've dug a little deeper. There are no doubt other feel-bad factors I have missed, and I may have doubled up a little in some ways but consider this a good start to your thinking. I was more than a little surprised how many quirks there are that conspire to give us a gloomy view of the world. Below is a summary of the feel-bad factors with a short description.

LIST OF ALL THE FEEL-BAD FACTORS

Information-gathering biases

Media biased for bad news: Bad news sells — we may have an evolutionary preference for bad news and media's aim is to sell, so that's what they give us.

Social media: It is easier now to compare ourselves to other people but only through polished/edited versions of their lives, so we probably feel worse about our situation.

Pervasiveness of advertising: Messages are shouted at us all the time, so we are encouraged to want more than we have.

Negativity bias: Bad things are more memorable from our daily lives — accidents, arguments, so our memories are more likely to be full of negative things.

Digital screen addiction: There is evidence that the always-on nature of information from screens make us feel less satisfied.

Thinking biases

We now have time to think: Hard problems of hunger, war, and plague are solved, so we have time to think about less significant issues — 'First World problems'.

Nostalgia bias: The past appears better than it actually was. We believe our childhood and early years were idyllic.

Confirmation bias: We continuously seek news to support current views, so it is hard to change how we perceive things.

Headwind/tailwind asymmetry: Things that help us seem invisible (e.g. the tailwind of stable, safe democracy), things that restrict our progress are top of mind (e.g. the headwind of fake news).

Availability heuristic: We remember stories about things we have recently heard more than data. This is not an inherently harmful thing, but when combined with bad news bias and confirmation bias, it exacerbates negativity.

Pessimism bias: We tend to think bad things are more likely to happen. This is probably a result of the cumulative effect of the other feel-bad factors.

Social expectation biases

Natural level of grumpiness: As a rule, grumping about things seems the norm and it is expected to give stories of how hopeless things are no matter how much things progress.

Explaining how good life is seems unpopular: Pointing out how great life is appears for some reason to be unpopular.

Cultural expectation of constant happiness: People are expected to be happy all the time but this is just not a realistic expectation, so we make an assumption it must have been better/easier in the past.

Need for social status: Everyone aiming for high social status is in a zero-sum game that not everyone can win.

Economic model biases

Economic models are wrong: Having experts tell you how bad things are when in fact they are not. The current models are not very good at the long-term analysis when goods and services change dramatically.

Nagging need for progress: As a society, we feel the need to continually make economic progress. As soon as we have one thing, we are thinking about the next thing, which is always some time in the future.

Economic inequality biases

Inequality seems so unfair: Other people seem to be doing way better — it just doesn't seem fair in a lot of cases.

Some people can't participate in society: Inequality means that some proportion can't join in with the rest of society. They just don't have the resources to be part of what everyone else is doing.

Belief in meritocracy: If you believe that your outcome in life is only related to your efforts, then you are likely to feel that any fault in doing badly is entirely yours.

This list can be thought of as a series of mini-flaws in the way we think or perceive things related to progress in the world. This list, in some ways, parallels the systematic flaws in thinking outlined in behavioural economics.

If you struggled with some of the comparonomic graphs in previous chapters, now is a good time to redraw them, knowing what you now know about feel-bad factors. These feel-bad factors cause real feelings, but it doesn't necessarily mean the feelings reflect reality.

ARE THERE ANY FEEL-GOOD FACTORS THAT ARE RELEVANT?

A long list of things that tend to make us feel life is not so good has been identified but it is worth asking if there are any feel-good factors that systematically make us feel good? I have struggled to find anything too significant. The optimism bias[1] is defined as the tendency to be over-optimistic, overestimating favourable and pleasing outcomes, but this is more focused on what we think will happen in the future rather than what we think about the past. It can also relate to information-gathering where we are more likely to remember praise than criticism, but it is perhaps the opposite for some people. Optimism bias has advantages in how it motivates us to do things that if we knew the amount of work at the start, we may not otherwise do, e.g. starting a company or writing a book ...

The other odd observation is that while it is common to talk about 'the good old days', it is also common for older folk to talk about how easier the young have it today. Back in my day, we had to work much harder; we didn't have inside toilets, we didn't go on fancy holidays, couldn't use calculators, had to use our brain. If you want a good laugh, the John Cleese sketch talking about the luxury of living in a cardboard box is worth a look.[2] So in a way, it is commonly acknowledged that things were harder back in the day but, gosh, they were still the good old days. I don't know quite what to make of this contrast.

There are most probably other significant feel-good factors but I've purposefully not spent time investigating these because they seem swamped by the feel-bad factors. I'd be interested to see anyone's comparable list if they can think of any.

HOW DO THE FEEL-BAD FACTORS INTERACT?

Some of the described feel-bad factors are probably more significant than others. Figure 35 shows the possible relative importance of some of the different feel-bad factors. This is a finger-in-the-wind kind of guess. I'm making the point that because I listed digital screen addiction, I don't think it is as important a feel-bad factor as the need for social status.

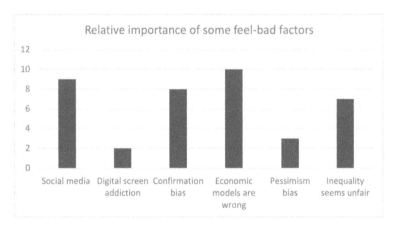

Figure 35 *A possible way to show the relative importance of some feel-bad factors.*

There is probably no correct way to rank the relative importance of the feel-bad factors, but the point here is to highlight that I think some of these are more important than others. There are many ways that the feel-bad factors can feed off each other. Steven Pinker provides an analysis of how the availability heuristic, bad news, and nostalgia bias link to reinforce the feeling that all is not well.

I have suggested that this can be attributed to three emotional biases that are baked into our psychology: bad dominates good, the illusion of the good old days, and moralistic competition. These feed into a single cognitive bias — the availability heuristic — which in turn interacts with the nature of news, thereby generating an inclination toward pessimism.[3]

CONCLUSIONS ABOUT FEEL-BAD FACTORS

Part Two of this book aims to answer the question 'Given life is so relatively good, why do we feel so bad?' At the start of this process, I thought I'd expand on the four or five well-known feel-bad factors, but was genuinely surprised that there seem to be so many quirks of the mind and social norms that make us feel bad about life. There are so many feel-bad factors, and they build on each other to almost guarantee our gut reaction to the state of the world will be gloomy. For anyone interested in why there may be so many feel-bad factors, I suggest you start with the book by Randolph Nesse *Good Reasons for Bad Feelings*[4]. While the book is primarily about extreme bad feeling associated with mental health, it outlines the evolutionary advantages of feeling bad.

Comparonomics is now defined as both the tools for working out our place in the world (comparonomic graphs) and the reasons why our perceptions are different (list of feel-bad factors). With this new set of tools and definitions, we now have a common language for thinking about how we can make life better.

If this book finished here, it would be useful, as it has created a tool that allows everyone to participate in a discussion on how things change. The analysis shows that overall we are much better off, and knowing this is a comforting thing, hopefully. Several genuine reasons why we might not feel so good about our current situation have also been highlighted. But now that we understand how we are getting on and why we often feel the opposite, it is time to think about what might make life even better.

PART III
HOW CAN WE DO BETTER?

13

CONVENTIONAL GOALS TO MAKE
LIFE BETTER

I HAVE OUTLINED how much better life is than 50 years ago covering both social and economic factors. A detailed and long list of genuine reasons why we don't feel so good about progress has also been defined. The last part of the book addresses the question: 'What could make life better?'

There are hundreds of possible things we could do to make life better, from serious government policies to mindfulness to practising silly walks. Let's dismiss the self-help type things and look at some policy objectives that are common goals of countries and governments around the world. I have chosen three common policy goals from across the political spectrum to look at whether they are likely to make a difference. This is a small subset of objectives that could be analysed, and I make no judgment on them being the most common or important. The ones I am going to examine are:

- Economic growth

- Decreasing inequality
- Improving social mobility.

Rather than talking about the messy specifics of how you might achieve economic growth, more equality, or social mobility, we just look at the high-level goal and ask: If we solved this, how would it change life?

Would improving economic growth, social mobility, or inequality change the feel-bad factors listed in the previous chapters and make us feel more satisfied with progress and life?

It is legitimate to ask whether it is a worthy goal to make people feel better about progress. Maybe the current level of angst is what drives us to make progress and, if we were more satisfied, progress would slow down. This seems to be something we can tackle at an individual level. If you don't want to feel better about the world, you can finish here, I guess. Maybe you can read on to see how to help other people feel better. As a point of clarification, I'm assuming that feeling better is a vital part of actually making life better.

I don't think that feeling better about things stops the striving to make things even better — otherwise, why write this book? If you can feel good along the way, rather than be angry at the crappy state of the world, that seems like a worthy objective. When this book was first conceived, I had the view that this sort of analysis would help identify which of the economic policies are likely to make the most significant impact. I didn't expect to show that many of the things we strive for don't look to make much difference at all. Even successful policy outcomes of economic growth, inequality, and social mobility may not change people's view of the world. It does not mean we should abandon them, as they have other benefits.

Table 1 shows possible policy solutions and indicates the impact they could have on the feel-bad factors. Light grey suggests they may have some effect and dark grey they may have a significant effect on the feel-bad factors. If there is nothing in the table, I assume they will not impact the feel-bad factor at all.

Table 1 visually shows the summary of the impacts, and it is surprisingly blank. So let's discuss each of the three policies and flesh out their effects on the feel-bad factors.

LIST OF FEEL-BAD FACTORS	Economic growth	Social mobility	More equality
Media biased for bad news			
Social media			░
Pervasiveness of advertising			
Negativity bias			
Digital screen addiction			
We now have time to think			
Nostalgia bias			
Confirmation bias			
Headwind/tailwind asymmetry			
Availability heuristic			
Pessimism bias			
Natural level of grumpiness			
Explaining how good life is seems unpopular			
Cultural expectation of constant happiness			
Need for social status			
Economic models are wrong	░		
Nagging need for progress	▓		
Inequality seems so unfair		░	▓
Some people can't participate in society			▓
Belief in meritocracy		░	

Table 1 How improving economic growth, social mobility, and more equality could impact the feel-bad factors. Light grey suggests a small impact, dark grey a significant impact, and blank no impact.

ECONOMIC GROWTH

Economic growth is something that most people agree is worth pursuing. I agree that the economic and technological progress over the last 200 years is the crucial reason that life is dramatically better. What is fascinating though is just how little pure economic growth affects the list of feel-bad factors identified in the previous chapters.

If we assume economic growth without changing equality, then obviously it will not affect the inequality feel-bad factors. Economic growth will not change any of the ways we gather information or the social expectations and thinking biases. Most of the things that cause us to believe there is not much progress are not affected at all by economic growth. I did not expect this when starting the analysis, though in hindsight it seems obvious.

The feel-bad factor that economic growth affects the most is our need for progress. More growth increases our sense of progress. Being told we are growing at 6% will feel better than being told we are growing at 1%.

It was thought that increased economic growth does not lead to much of an increased level of happiness and it even has a name. The Easterlin paradox is a concept in happiness economics. It is named after the economist Richard Easterlin, who suggested that a higher level of a country's per capita gross domestic product did not correlate with greater self-reported levels of happiness among citizens.[1] However, new analysis suggests that this is not necessarily the case and wealthier nations and citizens tend to be happier. Economic growth helps, but it does not solve all the feel-bad factors identified. You can hardly say on the face of it that the world is full of happiness and contentment despite an astonishing run of economic growth in the last 150 years.

Economic growth has proven to be a wonderful solution to pull people out of abject poverty, and we are well on the way to solving this. It is not necessarily logical to assume the same solution will address the next set of needs. It seems that this is not the case and we need to have a bit more of a think on how to resolve issues crucial to relatively affluent societies. To reinforce, I am not suggesting economic growth is wrong or bad. I am suggesting that it may not necessarily make us feel better and get to the root reason for dissatisfaction with life in general.

SOCIAL MOBILITY

Social mobility is a commonly desired political and economic goal, as it means that everyone has an opportunity.[2] It seems evident that equality of opportunity to improve your economic standing would help solve many of our problems. If everyone has a chance, it is a much fairer system. Often this social mobility is defined as the chance of someone from the lower economic quartile making it to the top economic quartile.

The term 'social mobility' has the implicit assumption that your social status is linked to your economic income. Let's assume this is the case; then it also implies that everyone in the lower quartile of income is of low social status and ditto high income equals high social status. By definition, there will always be the same proportion in the lowest quartile. Improved mobility gives some people a chance to escape low status but it also means others must fall into this lower social status. For every one that moves up, someone must move down.

Having high social mobility may even make social tensions worse because it will reinforce that if you have low social status, it is because of your skill and effort rather than poor luck, so you are looked down upon even more. The folks at the top with a higher chance of going down will also be more anxious. Changing social mobility does not fix the problem that people at the bottom feel inferior and those at the top feel superior. Richard Reeves makes an observation about the lack of social mobility in the US:

> For American society to work as it should, your children, some of them anyway, must be downwardly mobile.[3]

Let's have a look at how improved social mobility would impact the feel-bad factors in the previous chapters. Again, it seems that improving social mobility would not affect any of the factors related to how we gather information or how we think about that information. It is tempting to say it will help with the need for social status but in this definition, these are non-economic aspects of social status. Changing social status won't have any impact on the economic feel-bad factors, as it doesn't change economic models or change the nagging need for economic growth.

Improved social mobility could impact how we think about inequality. It won't stop the fact that certain people cannot participate, it'll just change the people that can and can't participate. Assuming that improved social mobility is a result of effort, then this reinforces the idea of a meritocracy where your reward is proportional to effort. This could, in theory, decrease the sense of hopelessness from being lower down the hierarchy. Improved social mobility would, however, increase the perception of fairness though; if you think back to the monkey experiment, seeing the other person being rewarded is still going to cause some angst.

Again, what seems surprising is that one of the holy grails of economic policy of improved social mobility would not make a significant impact on the core feel-bad factors that seem to make us dissatisfied.

It is worth noting that social mobility is also not an easy problem to solve. A recent study of tax records from Venice showed that the wealthiest families in 1427 are still the most affluent families now.[4] This sort of evidence reinforces the idea discussed earlier that pure meritocracy is a myth. Your economic status seems to have more to do with who your parents are than anything else. Other authors have noted that there are powerful incentives for those at the top to make sure that they never fall.

> The protections erected by the upper middle class mostly raise the share of income captured by the protected class, at the cost of both a smaller share for others and less growth overall.[5]

There are still lots of good things about improving social mobility. It seems to be a tough thing to solve but even if we did, it doesn't look to address some of the core issues that make us feel bad about life and progress.

MORE EQUALITY

There is a large quantity of evidence supporting the idea that inequality is increasing and that it is one of the most significant issues facing modern economies.[6] This is a topic that many folks have strong opinions on and even stronger views on how to address. Let's set these complications to one side and assume it was worth making society more equal and assume that we had achieved that without impacting too much else. Yes, I know these are giant assumptions, but we are using our imaginations here.

Now that we have solved inequality, how does it impact the factors that make us feel bad about life and progress? There are two things on the list that would be dramatically better. Obviously, inequality will not seem so unfair due to being a more equal society, and more people would be able to participate in more things.

Improving inequality also impacts other feel-bad factors like social media because it will not seem like you are missing out so much. Changing inequality will not impact the desire for social status because this is about non-economic aspects of social status. It's not going to improve other aspects of social status such as your chess playing if you are from Russia, singing ability if you are from Wales, or Morris dancing if you are English.

Again one of the most discussed and sought-after policy objectives does not seem to have solved many of the things on the feel-bad list. We would still be bombarded with bad news, grumble about lots of things, remember all the bad things that happen, pine for the good old days, and feel the nagging need for more.

There is no reason to think inequality is not a significant problem or that we shouldn't try to solve it. My point is that some other significant things make us feel bad about life and changing inequality will not impact these things.

CHAPTER SUMMARY

In summary, there are several policy objectives like economic growth, social mobility, and equality we strive for, with the view that it will make life better. The discussion in this chapter shows that these policies will not make much difference to the feel-bad factors that make us feel dissatisfied with life.

When I started this investigation, I certainly had a sense that conventional economic models were missing out on some significant measures of progress. It was a surprise how inaccurate these traditional models are. I knew I also wanted to document the other factors that cause us to feel so bad about progress. Again, I was astonished at the number of different feel-bad factors identified. The end goal from both those pieces of the investigation was to use this knowledge to work out what policy goals might have the most impact to make life better. I suspected it might be that inequality and social mobility are more significant than economic growth. I did not expect to find that none of these policies looks to make a massive difference. Even if we happened to be successful with all the policies combined, it wouldn't get to the root of what makes us feel dissatisfied with life.

I'm not sure if it is a standard process for authors to be surprised about their conclusions and insights after completing a project or whether they usually have a complete idea at the start and just go about describing it. For me, the process of writing and thinking about all these things has led to a number of these surprising insights. I may be a bit slow too, as it's taken me many years to come to these conclusions. Anyway, finding that many common policy objectives won't make much difference led me to think about what policies could make us feel better about our place in the world. Two following chapters branch off and do a deep dive into two new solutions.

In no way am I suggesting that economic growth, equality, or social mobility are bad things to try to achieve. The core message is that fixing these things alone will not get to the root of why so many folks feel bad about life and progress.

14
MODEL MANIA — BETTER MODELS OF HOW THE WORLD WORKS

Knowledge sets you free.[1]

THE FIRST NEW solution to allow us to feel better about life and progress is a little circular and obvious. A powerful antidote to feeling bad about progress is to be able to understand better why we feel like we do and to know that we are actually progressing quite well.

As discussed earlier, the application of inappropriate economic models gives the impression that many of us are not much better off than 50 years ago. However, the comparonomic graphs described in previous chapters plainly shows that we are doing quite well. Historically we are all in the 1% wealthiest that have ever lived. Even now, every time I think about this, it makes me feel grateful and hopefully it does for you too.

Knowing that life is vastly better would not necessarily help without also acknowledging the list of genuine feel-bad factors that cloud our judgments. Knowing the list of feel-bad factors helps, as it gives a perspective on the typical human feelings about such things.

If we have better models of the world, it will help. I use the word 'model' in this chapter to describe the following two things:

- Comparonomic graphs — ability to articulate more accurately how things compare over time.
- List of feel-bad factors — list of things you may not have previously been aware of that cause you to feel less satisfied with life.

Understanding both new models can have a high impact on how the feel-bad factors influence your daily life.

EXPERTS TELL US HOW TO THINK ABOUT THINGS — WHAT IF THEY ARE WRONG?

As described in Chapter 4 there is a commonly accepted narrative in the media that we are not doing so well. However, the comparonomic graphs show a different picture, so you can understand how well we are actually doing. Understanding this can give a sense of gratefulness that can make a significant impact on how we think about our place in the world. There are also some surprising other ways that this new understanding can make a very real positive difference in our day-to-day life.

CHANGE HOW WE THINK ABOUT STUFF

One thing we can do with this new appreciation of how well we are doing historically is to change our perception of the products we are continuously egged on to buy. Let's take the simple example of a smartphone. I used to be a slave to having the newest and best. Let's see how a comparonomic view of life could influence our decisions around this one simple example.

Harnessing your inner marshmallow resistance

You may have heard of the marshmallow experiment on children.[2] This was a series of studies on delayed gratification about 50 years ago by Walter Mischel. The children were offered a choice between one small reward provided immediately or two small rewards if they waited for a short period, approximately 15 minutes, during which the tester left the room. When they followed up, they found that children who were able to wait longer for the preferred rewards tended to have better life outcomes for the rest of their lives.

If you can delay your need for the latest and greatest phone features by as little as two to three years, you can get your phone for next to free. Remember this is a device that four to five years earlier was impossible for a billionaire to have. I now only buy lower-end phones that are second-hand, and they are typically a tenth the cost of the latest model. The last one I bought was about a year old, and it has lots of whizz-bang features my old one didn't. I'm sure I'm missing the most up to date features but I don't even know what they are. You can save yourself in the order of $500–1000 per year depending on how you look at it by harnessing your inner marshmallow resistance. A two or three year delay and you get almost for free something a billionaire four years earlier couldn't have!

It is worth dwelling on how astounding this is. It is not some inconsequential example but something people spend significant portions of their free time using. The most bewildering consequence of all is that the conventional way of measuring economic progress counts for almost nothing. If that is not an illustration of how inappropriate conventional economics is for measuring progress, I don't know what is.

It is not hard to imagine how you can amplify the phone example to several things about your life and suddenly you are vastly richer. Given the rate of change of technology, there has probably never been a better return on your ability to harness your inner marshmallow resistance.

Sometimes you don't even need to resist to get the same access as the wealthiest people in the world. If you think of entertainment and music, for a few dollars a week, you can have almost anything you want. As one example, Netflix spends billions of dollars a year on the best storytellers, actors, and production crews to create some astonishing entertainment. I suspect the wealthy watch the same shows because they don't have billions of dollars a year to make something even better just for them. Us regular folk may even enjoy this new form of high production quality, extended storytelling even more than the super-rich. Maybe the super-wealthy feel guilt given they have the option of flying off to watch some fantastic live play or concert, but we can sit back and enjoy the latest state-of-the-art entertainment.

Henry David Thoreau has a quote about how perception can change your view on wealth: 'A man is rich in proportion to the number of things which he can afford to let alone.' Unlike in the past, this does not involve significant sacrifice. You can still have things better than a billionaire, not by letting things alone, but delaying for a little bit.

Economic superheroes

So what do I think of the folk who buy the latest and the best smartphones? I love them. If they didn't exist, the rest of us couldn't have the advances in technology. Early adopters are the folk who pay a premium to test new things that if they are any good can be adopted by everyone. They are economic superheroes.

If you can afford to be an early adopter of something, please do, as you make it easier for all the rest of humanity. If everyone waited, the system wouldn't work. I was an early adopter of 3D printing that in hindsight cost me a small fortune. But if it weren't for folk doing this, new technology would never become available for everyone else. The money I saved using my inner marshmallow resistance on smartphones and other electronics allowed me to be an early adopter of electric cars, which have significant environmental benefits.

I suspect not all early adopting has the same level of public benefit. Being an early adopter of gold-plated toilets seems a bit of a stretch. I struggle to see why you would want one of these. I'm not sure there is a simple definition of the difference between things that may be beneficial to all and things that are silly excess, but I suspect most people can tell the difference without the need for formal definition.

The example of saving money on a smartphone may seem a little trivial but it can save you a lot over time. Having this understanding of our place in the world can have direct significant personal economic benefits. Think how much you could help by the simple gesture of sharing this book with your friends and family.

When you see someone who doesn't have the latest product, you can't assume they can't afford it and pity them. Maybe they have a stronger inner marshmallow resistance and have taken that saving to apply in different areas of their lives. Perhaps they have banked it in more time with their family and friends or some other passion of theirs. Pity can turn into admiration.

When you see someone with the latest thing that you may have an inner pang to have, you can be grateful for their willingness to pay for it so the rest of society can adopt it inexpensively. It will be next to free soon — yippee. Envy turns into gratefulness.

CHANGING HOW WE THINK ABOUT THE FEEL-BAD FACTORS

There are only a couple of the feel-bad factors that are not impacted by a better understanding of the comparonomic models. The first of these is a need for social status. Irrespective of knowing how well we are doing historically or how well you understand the other feel-bad factors, there will continue to be a need to feel respected from a social status point of view. No amount of feeling better about things in general will allow folks who don't have as much to be able to participate in activities in society.

Media bad news bias

Knowing how relatively good life is puts the constant bad news in media in perspective. Also knowing that there are substantial, rational reasons that the media is full of bad news is itself helpful. When you are aware of this bias for bad news, it does give a lot more perspective seeing the headlines and hearing the inevitable discussions that follow.

A practical antidote to bad news is reading hyperlocal news. These stories are generally more folksy and about minor community events rather than dark and disturbing. The reason for that is the reality that a lot of what happens around you is not dark and disturbing. The hyperlocal newspapers can't sensationalise, as people are too close to things. When the local news does get people upset about something, often with perspective, it falls into the 'high-quality problem'. 'Rubbish bins sometimes get full on busiest days of the year!' 'The beautiful old building hasn't been painted for 13 years and needs maintenance.'

Social media biases

Being aware that comparison is the thief of joy and some of the research on how people only post polished versions of their lives certainly changes how one views social media. When I do occasionally post things, I'm acutely aware that I don't want to cause envy because of what I post.

The other option is to opt out of surfing other people's social media posts. This is my preferred option, and I'm sure I miss out on some things because of it. But for the peace of mind and extra time I have, it seems like a good trade-off for me. I'm not suggesting you must reduce social media participation, as there are many benefits, but being aware of the issues will almost certainly give you a better perspective. Probably more experienced users understand these things, and it is more something that new users need to learn.

Advertising

Realising how well off we are helps reduce the pull of advertising for new things. It acts like a little relief valve for the constant demand to buy new things knowing you are already in the 1% from a historical point of view. Knowing how cheap some things are likely to become if you delay your gratification is also an antidote to the pull of needing the latest of everything.

Time to think bias

Thinking is so important,[3] but knowing the sorts of problems that we have had for most of history puts most of our 'high quality' problems into perspective. Being aware of this seems to be a little harder to put into practice in everyday life because of the immediacies of day-to-day problems. The dilemma of what subjects to choose for study as a student is, of course, a better problem than being hungry or attacked or ill, but it can still be a huge worry to select the right thing to do.

Nostalgia trap

The comparonomic models created show how much progress we have made. This means we can give up the idea that the old days were better than now. You can still look back fondly on your past but not wish to impose those conditions on the current generation.

Confirmation bias

Nothing helps this apart from maybe knowing about it. It is worth reminding ourselves of this one regularly as it has such an enormous impact on our ability to learn. This has been written about extensively elsewhere, so I won't expand on it here.

Headwind/tailwind asymmetry

I found this to be one of the more thought-provoking feel-bad factors. It is natural to feel hard done by. But you probably are not. I've certainly caught myself a few times falling into this trap, and again knowing about it gives perspective when this happens.

Natural level of grumpiness

The next time someone complains about how poor the service was at (insert hopeless company name), you can still participate and share your stories. It is part of social lubrication, but knowing how common and accepted this is will enable you to retain a little perspective. These familiar horror stories of how crap everything is are less likely to send you into a spiral of gloom. I still find it odd how much more usual grumbling seems to be than I was aware of previously. I don't think my social circles are particularly grumpy, it just seems to be part of the culture I happen to live in.

Positivity is unpopular

The unpopularity of positivity is one I struggle with a little bit still. I can't help myself when people talk about blatantly wrong things like the increased terrorist risk in Europe. I now, however, don't expect to be thanked for providing a more realistic view on this. I'm probably a little more tactful about how I have the discussions, and try to stimulate a debate around how good thing are compared to the past. Pointing out less risk from IRA or hijackings and letting them build on stories they know about gives them another perspective. If you point out blatantly they are wrong, then confirmation bias kicks in sharply and there is a risk you will be seen to be being a little arrogant (possibly true, so one needs to be aware).

Economic models are wrong

When you understand that we are the 1% from a historical point of view, you can dismiss the idea we are no better off than 50 years ago. Economic growth no longer seems the most important thing. If fixing an environmental or social issue impacts a little of economic growth, then it doesn't seem such an issue. I need to confess that I have environmental hippie tendencies from way back.[4] So many environmental issues don't get addressed primarily because of concerns about the economy. One of the reasons for writing this book is to try to give a more realistic perspective on the positive trends in the economy and why it is still normal to feel gloomy. Understanding this will hopefully allow everyone to prioritise other pressing environmental and social issues that need our attention.

Equality and fairness

The pang of unfairness of seeing others with something you can't have is still a real gut wrenching feeling. We seem to have evolved to feel unfairness so will certainly take some adjusting. The perspectives described above about delaying gratification and the fact that early adopters are economic superheroes help ease this envy. Also knowing you are in the historical 1%, for me at least seems to reduce the resentment of feeling like life is unfair.

Belief in meritocracy

Our discussion suggests that meritocracy is a myth or at best only part of the reason why people have different economic outcomes. The reason other people have more and are doing better is probably luck. Not much you can do about that, and knowing that helps.

Conclusions about better models

Understanding how the world works a little better is hardly a jaw-dropping solution. However, I suspect that next time you read a bad news headline, or someone complains about something, or they talk about the good old days, you will have a new perspective. It will probably mean you can participate a little more level-headedly and are unlikely to get angry at the world so much.

We shouldn't fool ourselves that knowing things is always going to make us feel better. As Daniel Kahneman points out in *Thinking, Fast and Slow*, knowing about flaws in how we think doesn't necessarily mean we will stop making mistakes. But it is a significant start.

When you compare how these more appropriate models of society impact the feel-bad factors, you can see how many are potentially improved. Table 2 shows which of the feel-bad factors are impacted by better models. It looks to have dramatically more impact than the more traditional objectives we aim for. Light grey suggests a small impact, dark grey a significant impact, and blank no impact.

LIST OF FEEL-BAD FACTORS	Economic growth	Social mobility	More equality	Better models
Media biased for bad news				■
Social media			▨	▨
Pervasiveness of advertising				
Negativity bias				■
Digital screen addiction				▨
We now have time to think				▨
Nostalgia bias				■
Confirmation bias				▨
Headwind/tailwind asymmetry				■
Availability heuristic				■
Pessimism bias				■
Natural level of grumpiness				▨
Explaining how good life is seems unpopular				
Cultural expectation of constant happiness				▨
Need for social status				
Economic models are wrong	▨			■
Nagging need for progress	■			
Inequality seems so unfair		▨	■	
Some people can't participate in society			■	
Belief in meritocracy		▨		▨

Table 2 How better models could impact the feel-bad factors. This looks to have dramatically more impact than the more traditional objectives we aim for.

This new understanding can cause you to have a significantly more favourable view of the world. The beautiful thing is that this is dramatically easier to achieve than improving economic growth, equality, or social mobility. You don't need to rely on politicians or officials to grind away at policy for years. TED founder Chris Anderson makes a good case for the power of better understanding:

> ... there are systemic flaws in the reported world view. Certain types of news — for example, dramatic disasters and terrorist actions — are massively over-reported, others — such as scientific progress and meaningful statistical surveys of the state of the world — massively under-reported. Although this leads to major problems such as distortion of rational public policy and a perpetual gnawing fear of apocalypse, it is also reason to be optimistic. Once you realize you're being inadvertently brainwashed to believe things are worse than they are, you can ... with a little courage ... step out into the sunshine.[5]

A point of caution about having this better understanding is that while it can be useful for you, how you communicate with others needs consideration. If someone is having what to them is a problem and you blurt out that it's just a natural level of grumpiness, you could come across as a bit of an arrogant knob. You have taken the time to understand and think about these things and know how common these feel-bad factors are. The associated feelings are real and normal, and it requires a little understanding when communicating about these things.

Having covered a relatively uncontroversial way to allow us to feel a little better about our place in the world, let's jump into something that may be a bit more contentious.

15

THE LAST GREAT 'ISM'

WHAT STRUCK me when thinking about the feel-bad factors was how many are related to our place, or perceived place, in society, i.e. how we compare to others. Ultimately this is not something that has any solution if everyone aspires to be at the top of the heap. It seems to me that a possible answer to this is to reject the idea of social status entirely. Let me define that a little before dismissing the idea. I'll then explain how social status could impact the feel-bad factors before discussing how we may go about removing the impact of social status. I am far from the first person to identify the issues with social status, but the novel thing I'm proposing below is how we may think of it and improve it in similar ways to how we tackle sexism and racism.

As society has evolved, we have mostly decided it is not okay to treat people differently based on their race, sex, religion, or sexual preference. Why is it okay to treat people differently based on their social status? Why should we bow down to people who happen to be kings, politicians, fast runners, wealthy, or good singers? What gives us the right to look down on people who do for us the many of the things we wouldn't like to do ourselves? Surely people are people, and we could treat them all the same? Hang on, you might say, social status is common to all societies and a natural part of human life. It's okay to look up to people who have achieved and look down on those that don't. Well, racism and sexism were universal too — it doesn't necessarily make it right.

DEFINITION OF STATUSISM

Let's define a new term, 'statusism,'[1] in a similar way to racism and sexism. It would be great if the word rolled off the tongue a little better but it seems like a useful parallel to racism and sexism, so let's go with it for now. Below is a definition of racism from the Oxford dictionary.

racism/ reɪsɪz(ə)m
noun

Prejudice, discrimination, or antagonism directed against someone of a different race based on the belief that one's own race is superior.

The belief that all members of each race possess characteristics, abilities, or qualities specific to that race, especially so as to distinguish it as inferior or superior to another race or races.[2]

Now let's parallel that definition for how we treat people of different social status.

*statusism/ statuss**ɪ**z(ə)m*
noun

Prejudice, discrimination, or antagonism directed against someone of a different social status based on the belief that one's own social status is superior.

The belief that all members of each social status possess characteristics, abilities, or qualities specific to that social status, especially so as to distinguish it as inferior or superior to other social statuses.

Instead of being racist or sexist you could be statist. Again, it doesn't roll off the tongue, but you get the idea. What I'm asking you to imagine is a world where you don't have to bow down to anyone, and you don't look down on anyone either. I've called this the last great 'ism' because it seems to me to be the last thing where it is socially acceptable to treat people better or worse due to some reasonably arbitrary label. Don't get me wrong; we haven't solved racism or sexism, let alone a bunch of others like ageism, fatism, speciesism or hipsterism.[3] With these other 'isms', most of us at least know that there is an issue and we should try to improve how we collectively treat people based on these things. However, it seems acceptable to worship at the feet of famous film stars, successful business people, champion sports stars, and awarded scientists. And some expect you to bow down to them too. Similarly, it seems acceptable to treat other folks almost as non-people ..., and they expect to be treated this way. What if people were just people that all deserved to be treated the same? This is not some communist or hippie ideology that everyone must have the same amount of stuff and achieve the same things, and everyone must be friends with everyone else. It is that irrespective of perceived social status, we treat everyone with the same human dignity.

Before discussing how we might reduce statusism, let us imagine we 'solved' it. Imagine there is no longer a need to 'keep up with the Joneses' because you don't feel inferior to those with more or superior to those with less. How would this impact the list of feel-bad factors from the previous chapters?

IMPACT OF SOLVING STATUSISM ON FEEL-BAD FACTORS

To start with, let's identify the feel-bad factors that probably don't have anything to do with social status:

- Media bias for bad news
- Negativity bias
- Digital screen addiction
- Nostalgia bias
- Pessimism bias
- Confirmation bias
- Natural level of grumpiness
- Explaining how good life is seems unpopular.

I don't think statusism can make much difference to these feel-bad factors but there are a number where it could make an impact.

Social media

If you don't give a damn about your place compared to other folks, then the social media impact of being able to see more people and seeing their polished lives will not make as much difference. I suspect you need to be proficient at not giving a damn about what other people possess to be able to quell the pangs of inadequacy that are common from social media. But it is possible.

Pervasiveness of advertising

If you stand back and look at most advertising, it has very little to do with significant benefits from a long-term perspective. A little-delayed gratification means you can have pretty much anything you want at a severe discount. Much of what we buy now serves to reinforce our social status and if we don't care, then the advertising doesn't have the same impact.

We now have time to think

Having time to think is a luxury with the perspective of the previous chapters. But using that time to sweat about how you compare to others should not be high on your list. Maybe you could even use the time to compare yourself to most folks that have ever lived and know that life is damn good. Knowing that you have from a historical perspective moved

on to high-quality problems helps reduce the need to keep
up with the Joneses.

Cultural expectation of constant happiness

One of the reasons for the expectation of happiness is that
this is what is expected by other people. If you are not
worried about your level of happiness compared to others
and are more aware that it is normal to have good and bad
days, then this reduces the impact of this feel-bad factor.

Need for social status

This one is easy. If you don't feel the need to bow down to
anyone or look down on anyone, then you will be free from
social status anxiety.

Economic models are wrong

This is another feel-bad factor where the reduction in
statusism makes a subtle improvement. If economic models
tell you are not doing that well and you care about your
status relative to folks in the past, then it has an impact. If
you don't care about your status and you know that you are
doing better than most people that have ever lived, then
again inappropriate economic models have less impact.

Nagging need for progress

I suspect knowing about this learned need to continually
make progress is more important than solving statusism.
However, even at a national level, reading about other
countries with higher growth rates seems to make some folk
feel the need for their country to be doing better. This is like

social status of the whole country, and it can be dismissed by not giving a damn.

Inequality seems so unfair

It seems unlikely that life will feel so unfair if you don't bother comparing yourself to others. The previous chapter discussed some other ways you can think about folks that have better or more stuff than you do. This will reduce our primal tendencies for envy.

Some people can't participate in society

My initial thought on this feel-bad factor is that statusism won't affect the reality of people not being able to participate. However, there are some ways that this could make a difference. As a trivial example, if you invite folks around for a meal and serve them caviar and champagne, but they can't afford to reciprocate, it's likely to put a dampener on future social gatherings. Not that we need to investigate people's relative means before interacting, but being aware of some of these things could make it possible for more people to participate in more activities.

Belief in meritocracy

If we don't care about our place in the world compared to others, then we won't care about how people happened to get there whether by chance or effort.

CHAPTER CONCLUSIONS

In this chapter, I have suggested the mental leap that we discard the notion of social status and treat everyone with the same dignity. If we did this, then it would have an impact on many of the things that make us feel bad about life. Table 3 shows how many of the feel-bad factors are impacted compared to some of the standard policies we pursue. Again, dark grey indicates a significant impact, light grey small impact and blank means no impact.

Changing how we think about social status could make a significant impact on how we feel about life. When combined with the improved models of social progress, then these two new solutions look to cover a lot of the feel-bad factors. I realise that a discussion on changing how we think about social status may seem a little hippie for a proper economics book — if you think that now, just wait for the next chapter.

What I have tried to do is build the case that life is better than we may think. I have shown there are real reasons why we feel worse about progress. Like all economists, I'm looking for ways to improve these things. Standard objectives like strengthening economic growth, inequality, and social mobility don't seem to make much of a difference. Having an improved understanding of models of these things helps dramatically as the previous chapter showed, but changing how we think about social status seems to make a big difference too.

LIST OF FEEL-BAD FACTORS	Economic growth	Social mobility	More equality	Solving statusism
Media biased for bad news				
Social media			▨	■
Pervasiveness of advertising				■
Negativity bias				
Digital screen addiction				
We now have time to think				▨
Nostalgia bias				
Confirmation bias				
Headwind/tailwind asymmetry				▨
Availability heuristic				▨
Pessimism bias				▨
Natural level of grumpiness				
Explaining how good life is seems unpopular				
Cultural expectation of constant happiness				▨
Need for social status				■
Economic models are wrong	▨			
Nagging need for progress	■			
Inequality seems so unfair		▨	■	
Some people can't participate in society			■	■
Belief in meritocracy		▨		■

Table 3 *How solving statusism could impact the feel-bad factors.*

What was analysed in this chapter is the idea of rejecting social status altogether. I asked you to imagine if we didn't care about social status, and showed it would reduce the impact of a lot of the feel-bad factors. The harder job is to work out how we could achieve this and whether it is worth doing. I suspect you will not be surprised to know that this is the subject of the next chapter.

16
STATUSISM — CHANGING HOW WE THINK ABOUT SOCIAL STATUS

Striving for social status is a universal goal that not everyone can win. The discussion in this chapter is relevant to my personal social settings and they will not be universal to all the cultures represented by the middle billion. Hopefully, it gives you an inkling of how embedded some expectations around social status behaviour are. There are a few stories about how you can push these social expectations and become a little freer from the confines of social status.

WHAT IS SOCIAL STATUS AND HOW DO YOU GET IT?

The discussion below mostly applies to the social status that we get because of the type of work that we do. A brain surgeon is considered differently from the person who cleans the bathroom in a hospital. You can also have social status due to a myriad of other things such as good looks, ability to sing or play sport, and much of the discussion is equally valid for this type of social status too. We derive such a large part of social status from our vocation that I want to focus mostly on this aspect of it.

If you think of the 'low status' jobs, they are typically things we would not like to do ourselves. If you think of the 'high status' jobs, they are typically more stimulating and enjoyable. Should we treat 'high status' folks better because they have a more enjoyable job? This seems a bit weird and arbitrary. Sure, the higher status jobs may be harder to do but we would probably all prefer to do them given a choice. We probably wouldn't want to do low-status jobs so shouldn't we treat these people even better? Well, in general, we tend not to.

IS SOCIAL STATUS JUSTIFIED?

The most significant difference between statusism and things like racism and sexism is that it is not mostly fixed at birth. You can change your social status but not as easily your race or gender. If you climb up and achieve great things, then maybe you deserve to be fawned over; if you are too lazy to make anything of yourself, then perhaps you also deserve to be overlooked. Because there is a level of self-determination, should it make any difference? The discussion on meritocracy gives some evidence that it is not all up to your efforts but, even if it is, does that change anything?

Remember, social rank is a system where not everyone can win despite everyone's efforts. It is a mathematical certainty that half of us will be below average, however you define average. Beware the politicians promising the majority of people can do better than average. Only 10% of people can be in the top 10% no matter how you define 'the top'. The only thing you can change is how you treat people in these different layers of status. Independent of whether the status is based on sporting, intellectual, income, or looks, you can acknowledge that they are all just people getting by.

Social hierarchy is something common to most cultures and has been written about for thousands of years. According to Plato, slaves had bronze in their souls; rulers, a group of philosopher kings, were men with souls of gold. Because we have done it for ages doesn't mean we shouldn't question it.

The first reaction when challenged on something like this is to reject it. Of course, I should treat a billionaire better than someone who makes my coffee. Why? You can still appreciate a billionaire's skill and dedication without bowing down to them. If there were one of these two you should bow down to, it would surely be the one who is happy to wake up each day and come in to make a beautifully crafted coffee for you. But I don't suggest you bow down to them either — just treat them the same.

One way to think about whether social status is justified is to put yourself in the shoes of those who don't happen to have the skill set to thrive in a modern economy. Given the fact that you have got this far through the book, you are probably doing all right in that you have time to read, money to spend on books (or skills to pilfer a free version), time to think, and ability to reason around complex issues. I guess that you may well have a few skills to cope with the way modern society has evolved. I can admit I happen to have an appropriate set of skills that makes it easy for me to thrive. There is, however, an extensive range of things I suck at. If chance had conspired that these skills were the ones that determined my place in the world, it would be a bit daunting.

If we take an example of one of the many things that I'm horrendously bad at — singing. No quantity of beer can dull the looks of horror on peoples' faces when I try to sing. Even the word 'karaoke' sends shudders down my spine. I can't imagine how unpleasant life would be if people judged me only on my singing ability. What if you woke up one day without the skills to have a high-status job — would you be any less of a person? The skills required to thrive in a modern economy is a moving beast and an oddly random set of skills. I sometimes wonder how my scrawny genes made it through times when brawn was critical. If you happen to have skills that allow you to thrive in the current economy, there is no guarantee it will last forever so it is worth thinking about how we can make it possible for everyone to live with dignity.

GAMES YOU CAN PLAY

In this section, I'll explain how you can play with some accepted norms around social status. A few things that we do without realising are directly related to standard behaviour about social status. I'm not suggesting you repeat these because some are awkward, but it does make you realise how baked in our perceptions about social status are.

What do you do?

One of the most common questions people ask when meeting others is 'What do you do?' Because of the quirky nature of what I do, I can honestly answer a range of things from 'unemployed' to more 'acceptable' answers. I thought I'd like saying 'unemployed', but it can end up being rather awkward. On answering 'unemployed' on a country entry form, I had a customs officer tell me I didn't look unemployed. I couldn't help but ask him what unemployed people look like. This is not a high-quality strategy for getting through customs quickly. Apparently, because I'm not in a paid job now doesn't mean I'm unemployed — I had worked out by then the only acceptable answer to that was 'Okay, sir.'

Saying you are unemployed is also an awkward answer when you meet new people because I think you are supposed to say, for example, you are a builder in between jobs. Unemployed is not an acceptable answer. Try it if you want to kill a conversation. I do understand that it could be a question about what interests you but at the moment your value seems to be tied up to what your job is.

I'm not assuming that telling people you are unemployed in any way lets me understand the real hardships of actually being unemployed. The point is to understand a little of how people perceive each other via the status of what they do.

In the presence of a high-status person — purposefully spend time on other people

Another thing I've been experimenting with is how to interact with people when you meet them. For a quirky reason, I happen to have a reasonable number of chances to meet people of high social status but am lucky enough that I don't need anything from them, so I can be a little experimental (think high-level government/business folks). Different status is most noticeable when you meet two or three people at the same time, a high-status person and their 'minders' or 'underlings'. After being introduced to the two or three people, you are expected to direct your first social interaction at the high-status person. I've been actively directing it at the lowest social status person, and the uncomfortableness is evident and amusing (to me anyway).

The first reaction is to try to direct the conversation back to the important person in case I don't realise the social hierarchy here. You may only have a few moments with this important person, so you should make the most of interacting with them! But I just met two people I want to talk to. I can choose who I will talk to first. I'm not ignoring the other one, just directing first interaction in what conventionally seems wrong.

As part of social niceties, you often start with a comment about something trivial like the weather, traffic, or local events. Even directing these questions at the underlings is deemed inappropriate but it is significantly amplified if you ask their opinion on something important about which the high social status person knows a lot. It becomes painful ...

'Don't you realise I'm not the one with important opinions?' The funny thing is often the opinions of the important person are known, and I'm more interested in what the other people around them think, though I know they probably couldn't offer a free answer in the presence of the high-status person. This hierarchy is so in-built that these types of interactions are awkward for everyone. Maybe it's not as bad as back in the day talking to 'the help' or slaves, but still surprising how uncomfortable little twists in social norms can be.

I have heard that if you are the person of the highest social status, this can be viewed differently (I'm not of high social status to try it, sorry). Charismatic leaders are known for choosing people in the background to pull into the conversation to make them feel important and show inclusion. But if you are not the top dog and you decide to do this, you would probably be considered a social pariah. Imagine Bill Clinton picks you as a relatively unimportant person in the room to talk to, and you come up and choose to continue the conversation with his assistant.

The other common time you meet people of different social standings is when the high social status person is with their husband/wife/partner. On meeting a high social status male and his wife, I initiate the central conversation with his wife. If it goes on too long, it is deemed very inappropriate, but the other way around would be perfectly fine. It is appropriate to include the partner a little but certainly not as the primary focus. No wonder we see so many bored partners wandering around social gatherings.

The same is true if I meet a high social status female and then initiate and continue the conversation with her husband. I've only done this once because it was too uncomfortable. The daggers from the high-status female and her husband made me think they both thought I was sexist not wanting to talk to a woman first. This is not the case; I thought I'd not follow the social norms and direct more of the conversation to the relatively low social status person.

I'm not suggesting you do this but the point is to show you some of the things you can play with to test how strongly social status is tied into the expected ways we behave.

Are you busy? Why would I want that?

One of the most common questions people seem to ask each other is 'Are you busy?' It's an odd question. I tried answering 'no' for a while, and most of the time people would ask if I was okay. It could be an invitation to tell people 'How important are you?' but more probably it's a general kind of asking 'How are things going with work?'

It is also odd because often we complain about not having enough time for all the things we want to do. Yet the most socially accepted thing is to be busy all the time. Maybe it is some hangover from a Protestant work ethic that you are supposed to work hard to be a good person. And if you can't or aren't, then you are not a good person?

This could all sound a bit high and mighty as there are folks working three jobs that would love not to be busy. Lots of people also make themselves perpetually busy as a badge of honour. An alternative is to take some perspective and understand that by any historic standards we are all quite wealthy. Most of what we 'need' to buy these days is about keeping up with others around us. You can opt not to care as much about that and make your life less busy if you choose.

Maybe asking how busy you are doesn't have as much to do with social status. My standard answer now to 'Are you busy?' is typically something like 'Not really — I think busy is a bit overrated' or 'Why would I want to be busy?' Maybe I'm reading too much into what is a socially typical way to check in on how things are going.

Change your appearance and watch the difference

A simple way to see the difference appearance can make is to see how differently you are treated in a hardware store if you are wearing a suit versus a high-visibility jacket and work boots. This is a hard experiment for me due to my aversion to suit wearing and my frequent visits to the local hardware store where they mostly recognise me (yes, I have genuine 'stuff' weaknesses too). You can understand that the folks serving you will assume you have more knowledge about what you want when wearing working clothes but there is also a change in tone like you are one of us. What I found more surprising is how much more likely you were to be acknowledged and have conversations with the other people wearing work clothes. Maybe there is nothing inherently wrong with any of that as it speeds up information transfer but the fact that you are treated so differently based on perceived social class is quite ingrained.

These stories don't prove anything about statusism but are intended to get you to think about different embedded layers of social status expectations in social interactions.

Actively engage those that may be deemed to have lower social status

It is easy to slip into the social norm of ignoring some folk. While queueing at a busy international airport bathroom recently (clearly not in first-class lounge …), I noticed how people mostly ignored the person with the rather grim job of trying to keep everything stocked and clean. Almost no one acknowledged their efforts but when you think about it, we should be deeply appreciative. Imagine if they weren't there. Even if you don't speak their language, it is not hard to look them in the eye, smile and let them know you appreciate what they are doing. From one person to another, many thanks. While this is hardly going to make their day and could be a pain if everyone did the same thing, I've always received a smile back. Irrespective of perceived social status, I suspect everyone likes to be acknowledged and appreciated. It's not hard to do.

For folks you see regularly, there is no excuse for not knowing their name and over time being able to have some friendly social banter. An easy test of this is when you walk into your coffee shop (or equivalent), are you greeted with a smile or indifference? The answer is probably more of a reflection on you. I haven't found many grumpy folks you can't turn over time, and it's entirely fine if they choose perpetual grumpiness too, just not because of the way you interact with them. This doesn't imply I think folks that work in coffee shops are lower social status. We all have some micro social status hierarchies going on. Try asking a barista for a triple shot, decaf latte with whipped cream and cinnamon on top and I suspect you may get a sneer of contempt (I'm going to say in this case it may be deserved).

Throughout history, there have been different versions of this quote from J.K. Rowling: 'If you want to see the true measure of a man, watch how he treats his inferiors, not his equals.'[1] You would think I'd like this quote and I mostly do, but other people are not inferior — they are just people.

Treating people the same doesn't mean being disrespectful

This discussion on how people should be treated the same doesn't mean you must throw out the idea of respect. When one is invited to Buckingham Palace to have tea with the Queen, I don't suggest you greet her by saying 'Yo, Queenie — what up, girlfriend?' A polite level of respect is all that everyone deserves. I'm sure the Queen is lovely, but probably no lovelier than the folk serving the cucumber sandwiches.

Poke fun at ridiculous status things

Some things are comically absurd when it comes to folks' desire for status.

> At the luxury end of the market, water has become more like wine, argues Michael Mascha, the author of a guide to fine water. In expensive restaurants the precise origin of water is what matters; many eateries offer water lists along with the wine selection. For power-lunchers in

health-conscious Los Angeles, says Mr. Mascha, buying an expensive bottle of water is a way to signal status.[2]

It's fricken water!

Talking about wine, do you know why wine competitions are often split into price brackets? Because if they don't, the cheap wines can win top prizes. Famously, a bottle of chardonnay with the endearing nickname 'two-buck-chuck' for its low price beat 2300 other wines[3] to win the supreme award. Real blind taste tests suggest that expensive wines don't taste better than cheap ones.[4] I don't recommend pouring cheap wine into an expensive bottle and having wine aficionado friends rave about it. I did this once but didn't have the heart to tell them they were drinking cheap wine. I've saved a lot of money on wine with this too. I'm not trying to be a killjoy here. If this is your passion and it brings you joy, go for it. Just don't kill yourself to buy expensive wine to impress other people.

It is not hard to take some of your favourite expensive indulgences and get someone to do a proper blind taste test for you — wine, chocolate, beer, or cola. But then if you can afford it, there is no high crime involved so indulge away. But you also have the option of something as good without the social status, and you can use your newfound wealth on anything else you wish (or bank some freedom). But what will people think if you don't have the right brand of things? Well, this is one of my all-time favourite quotes from Winston Churchill:

When you're 20, you care what everyone thinks, when you're 40 you stop caring what everyone thinks, when you're 60 you realize no one was ever thinking about you in the first place.

I suspect most people you interacted with today will not lie in bed tonight thinking about all the brands of products they saw you with. Maybe there are some people that do that but not many, surely? Dare I suggest if you know people like this, you may want to find other folks to hang out with?

A WORD ON THE 1% OF THE 1%

If you happen to be in the top 1% earners today then historically you are the 1% of the 1%. For every 10,000 people that have lived, you are the top one — the top 0.01%. Let me be so bold as to make a few suggestions on how you may make the most of your extreme good fortune. First — pay your taxes. Most of you do, but for those who try to dodge through tax havens, you are most likely going to be named and shamed at some stage. The Panama and Pandora Papers will just be the start and it seems clear that society does not deem this acceptable. Yes, it may be legal but the only reason for not paying tax is to increase your ranking/status spot within the top 0.01%. How could this 'benefit' compare with being named alongside drug dealers, corrupt government officials and other criminals? It is perfectly legal to be an arsehole but I wouldn't recommend that either.

On a more productive note I'd be prepared for the question 'What are you doing to help the world with your fortunate position?' This is something we should all ask of those more fortunate. Despite the fact we have made so much progress, a mountain of problems still need to be solved. It doesn't mean you have to switch your life from earning to giving like Bill Gates. Elon Musk has a great answer pursuing a purely commercial path to make the world greener, safer and bigger (space). In both these cases I can see huge social benefits in what they are doing. As someone of wealth, you have more freedom to be innovative to make a difference. Don't do it so people pat you on the back. Do it because most that do, tend to report it is more rewarding than anything else you can do.

WILL SOCIETY CHANGE? CAN WE SOLVE STATUSISM?

The reason I like the term 'statusism' is that it covers the whole range of things that give people social status — job, wealth, where born, what family, where you live, how intelligent, how hardworking, how attractive, how many fast twitch muscles you have. The way to solve statusism is to throw the whole lot in a big pot and reject the lot.

Statusism is tightly embedded in culture such as movies, TV, and music so it feels like it would be hard to change. Well, sexism, racism, and homophobia were all baked in too, so there is some hope for change. What is particularly encouraging is that the speed of change seems to be accelerating. Homosexuality seems to have gone from a mostly criminal activity to widely accepted much faster than it took for similar progress on sexism and racism (yes, still lots of progress to make on these too). If we think about the stages society goes through in this transition, maybe it involves the following steps. I'll illustrate with racism:

- Acknowledging that racism is a bad thing.
- Trying not to be racist yourself.
- Pointing out to other people that racism is not acceptable or appropriate.
- Maybe laws change to make it illegal.
- It becomes more broadly socially unacceptable where you wouldn't think to be openly racist.
- Language changes to reflect the new norms.

These stages are not a thorough list or a linear progression, and obviously, we still have a long way to go with racism and sexism. For statusism, I suspect we are still at the first step. Is bowing down to people or looking down on people based on social status acceptable? Should I be able to treat certain folks in society like an inferior underling? Should I be expected to fawn over people that can run fast, or sing well, or work out a way to make lots of money? Obviously, I think these are ideas we need to discard. I guess that first part of the debate is the hardest but it starts there. Of course, we shouldn't pay women as much as men, they are not as good. Of course, we should treat homosexuals differently, they are morally depraved. Of course, we should treat Arabs with suspicion. Of course, billionaires are more important than aged care workers.

If you agree and think we should ditch the idea of social status altogether, then below are some next stages that naturally follow:

- Try not to treat people differently at a personal level. Bow down to no one — look down on no one. This does take some practice, but from my little experiments, I don't see too many downsides ... and lots of upsides.
- Try not to seek status yourself — this can be a lot harder thing to do.
- Point out to others that it is not cool to be statist. I have an old pet peeve of mine that is now amplified. Dining with people who are unnecessarily rude to waiters winds me up even more than it used to. These people happen to be running around organising our food. You should probably be incredibly grateful, and there is no excuse to think you are better than them and be rude to them. Sure, sometimes shit happens but forgetting a side of mustard is hardly grounds for a telling off.
- Maybe there will be laws changed? The beautiful thing about trying to change statusism is that we don't need laws modified to get most of the benefits (none that I can think of anyway).
- Language will evolve. Maybe words like 'lower class' become as socially unacceptable as 'homo', and 'housewife'? Now, that is a big leap but who knows.

It is never easy to change habits formed over generations. Malcolm Gladwell explained in his book *Blink*[5] how hard it is to not be racist even if you genuinely think you are not. There is a survey[6] you can do to test yourself, and it is frustrating that even if you don't want to have biases, they seem hard to shake. I suspect if you are like me, sometimes you will slip up and flip into a mindset that is too judgmental of others. I've found it a wonderfully freeing experience knowing that I don't have anything to prove to anyone and can more meaningfully enjoy the company of more people than I used to.

LANGUAGE MATTERS

The easiest way to show you that language matters is to say 'faggot', 'homo', 'nigger', or 'slut'. I'm guessing at least some of these words make you feel uncomfortable. Now, these words are in the extreme but as attitudes change, the acceptable language changes too. Try referring to a woman as a housewife or 'sweetie' and see how you get on. It wasn't that long ago that this was completely acceptable. Let's think of some phrases that may not last if we reject the idea of statusism:

- Upper class — this term assumes that this group is superior to others. They are not.
- Working class — this implies some people work and others don't. While it used to refer to physical labour, it has increasingly switched to include service work. It mostly, however, implies lower

social class that is in some way inferior to others. They are not.

- Underclass — is a horrific term with an added implication that people are inferior, and they always will be. Nope, we can't assume that.
- Middle class — yes, I even dislike this seemingly innocuous term because it implies some people are superior to them, and some are inferior. They are not.
- Ruling class — some people are better at setting rules for other to follow. Nope, they are not.
- Class struggle — people of different groups must fight each other to make their way in the world. No, they don't (sorry, Marx).
- Class/social mobility — this implies a hierarchy where some type of people or jobs are more important than others, and you can move up or down the hierarchy. You can reject the hierarchy too.

I'm not saying we shouldn't be able to talk about these things but more that we shouldn't label people and discuss the world in terms that have implied meanings that I don't think are right. I used the term 'middle billion', so maybe that is as bad? I purposely don't use the term 'middle class' because that has all sorts of associated baggage. There are people with different incomes, but I do not comment on their social class. We all know from people we have met that your income level is not a good judge of character. You can still discuss economic mobility, but you don't need to imply a value judgment about social status by calling it 'social mobility'.

I suspect it may be useful to reject some of these terms that have inappropriate social status baggage embedded with them. Don't expect it to happen any time soon. It is, however, something you can be more aware of when discussing these subjects.

NO DOWNSIDES TO REJECTING SOCIAL STATUS PERSONALLY

Having lived this new perspective on life for a while now, I'm not sure that it has many disadvantages. I probably have a more meaningful relationship with some folk I may not have been as conscious about interacting with in the past. I don't feel intimidated when I meet anyone. They're just people who have their good days and bad and irrespective of their 'status'. I'm no longer trying to impress anyone. I'm more grateful for all that I have but it doesn't mean I curl up in a ball of uselessness. The work I'm involved in is going better than ever, and I don't miss the extra income and status from doing something with higher status. I would have never otherwise had the time and freedom to fully develop these theories that have been brewing for a long time but I was always too busy doing 'proper' things. My lack of chasing status means I've had time to think and put the theory down in detail.

POLICY IMPLICATIONS FOR COMPARONOMICS

It is common that a new theory in economics will then lead to policy recommendations to make the world better. What we are suggesting here are some different policy goals rather than specific policies. Policy is typically about how to achieve something, not about deciding what is worth achieving. For example, Solow[7] and Romer's[8] economic growth theory led to policy recommendations that emphasise the value of stimulating research and development to achieve economic growth. Schumpeter's theories emphasise the importance of policies that encourage entrepreneurs to stimulate creative destruction.

More recently, behavioural economics theories created 'nudge units'[9] around the world that use their insights to get better outcomes. Another recent example is Piketty's work on inequality and the proposed solution of a comprehensive capital tax. His analysis shows that wealth is self-reinforcing due to returns on capital being higher than economic growth, so wealth concentrates over time.[10] His proposed solution is a capital tax to bring the net return below economic growth, so it is no longer naturally self-reinforcing. Given how mobile capital is, it is hard to imagine any policy harder to implement. If one country introduced this sort of tax, the capital could flow out of one country and flow to another with lower tax. Maybe we get all countries to introduce the policy at the same time. It is difficult to imagine anything less likely than that.[11]

Comparonomics is a new theory mostly about how to change your perception of the world. It seems we are progressing quite well and have a clear understanding of why; despite this we often still feel bad. My guess is that you can gain 50–70% improvement by changing your personal view on these things. This percentage improvement is a complete guess based on no empirical evidence. The nice thing though is there is no need to lobby and get political change but to change your view on life. I suspect that if enough people reject statusism and understand how well we are doing, then the other 50–30% of the benefits could be made without the need to lift a legislative pen. If we look at how changes in attitude to racism, sexism, and homophobia have propagated, this does not seem entirely out of the question — indeed, a little more likely than a global wealth tax.

Keeping the issue of inequality in mind that Piketty raised, it may well be that changing attitudes on social status may be the driver to then make more progressive taxation socially acceptable. If one country changes their attitude to statusism, then they could implement a more progressive tax structure without the flight of capital. Folks could be more relaxed about such things. I'm not saying that is likely, but it seems more likely than a global wealth tax independent of changing attitudes to social status.

I suspect that a problem with this view on policy is that it will sound a bit too hippie to be taken seriously.[12] If the end analysis of this book had concluded that we need to increase quantitative easing or tax capital flows, it would appear more like proper economics. Remember, I have taken the broad definition of economics as trying to understand our place in the world and how to make it better. While our solutions may not sound as technical, it is more empowering because it is in your control. You don't need to wait for anyone else, and it's possible to see a way that this enhanced view of life could propagate and make life better for everyone.

LEFT RIGHT OUT

Now for the hard bit that you may have already made your mind up on. Is this theory right wing or left wing? The 'right' might love it because:

- It demonstrates that even the poor are better off than the rich from not many years ago in many ways. So maybe they should be satisfied with their lot and should stop trying to take money off the ones that create it (please don't interpret it like this!).
- There is a suggestion that early adopters of the latest and greatest gadgets do the general population a service.
- Economic growth as measured by speed of economic progress is going even better than other models suggest, so let's keep on going.

The folk on the 'left' may love the theory because:

- It argues we shouldn't treat the rich better than the poor.
- That economic growth may not be the most important solution for a better society.
- If the speed of economic progress is an important goal, then the natural end game from this line of

STATUSISM — CHANGING HOW WE THINK ABO... 203

thinking is a more equitable society (speed of
making new things available to all).

- The phrase 'Make America Great Again' seems like
complete nonsense when you understand the
progress we have made. If you want to make
America more like the past, then a more accurate
description could be 'Make America More Racist,
Sexist, Homophobic and Poor Again' — maybe too
much for a bumper sticker?

- There is a good framework for the progression of
liberal ideas' rejection of racism, sexism, and
homophobia.

Well — there may well be more than two ways to look at the
world. Creatures as complex as humans don't have to fit
nicely into old random ideas that are more than a little dated.
I can admit to never being overly political and seeing
sympathy with both sides of this arbitrary split in
worldviews. Because this theory doesn't sit nicely in either
camp, I suspect the hardcore on both sides will reject it. My
aim wasn't to strengthen either side of the left/right political
spectrum but to try to learn something new and useful. I
have faith that there are enough folks with open enough
minds to take something useful out of this irrespective of
political ideology.

CONCLUSIONS ABOUT HOW TO CHANGE
STATUSISM

This chapter is a little bit personal as it describes some
experiments with the idea of rejecting social status. The

short conclusion is that from an individual point of view, it seems to work well independently of what anyone else does. It may be that striving for social status is the incentive that has kept us on track to continually improve life. Will Storr's book *The Status Game* describes just how pervasive chasing status is in life and thinks that 'The joy of status is nature's bribe that tempts us into being useful.' I strongly suspect I've been more productive since rejecting social status, not that productivity is the most important thing anyway. Changing our views on social status also doesn't seem nearly as hard as some of the other proposed solutions to the world's problems.

SUMMARY AND CONCLUSIONS

In economics, there isn't one 'right' answer that stays right forever, like in a maths problem ...[1]

THE POINT of this book is to see if we can learn something new about the human condition with the view to make our lives better. To build this story, I ask three simple questions that formed the three parts of the book:

- How are we doing?
- How do we think we are doing?
- How can we do better?

While they are simple questions, they are quite broad. I purposefully made them manageable by sidestepping the problematic issues of why things have changed and how they are likely to change in the future.

The first part of the book started with a simple 'How are we doing? How is life progressing?' Our solution is a new tool called a comparonomic graph that allows anyone to work this out themselves. The positive direction of most progress is encouraging.

The tool also shows how poor conventional economics is at measuring change in progress over time. Ambitiously, I designed an alternative form of economic growth theory that considers the speed that new goods and services become available to everyone. By this new measure, economic progress has never been faster.

Part Two of the book investigated how we think we are doing. I leveraged the work behavioural economists have done that show systematic quirks in our perceptions that may not always be in our best interests. A list of 20 feel-bad factors was defined that systematically make us feel worse about progress and life in general.

My goal in this investigation is to work out some policy recommendations to make life better. The surprising thing is that some of our most common policy objectives like economic growth, social mobility, and equality don't get to the root of our dissatisfaction. The two new solutions are less technical, more personal and don't need legislation. One is being aware of more useful models of the world, and the other is the idea of entirely rejecting social status.

> ...part of Marshall's original dream [was] of economists seeking not merely to apply their ideas in a worldly way,

but to produce both better ideas and, in the end, a better world. [2]

SUMMARY OF PART ONE

How are we doing?

Comparonomic graphs are a new useful tool for understanding how life changes over long time periods. Anyone can actively participate in a meaningful discussion about how things change rather than defer to 'expert' theories and detailed modelling with hidden assumptions. The comparonomic analysis is accessible to everyone, therefore empowering and enabling a change in perspective. This tool gives dramatically different results compared to conventional economic analysis. It shows the mountain of wealth King Louis supposedly has, is a desert of poverty when comparing the details of life that are important to most people (Figure 36).

The more relevant question is to investigate how our life compares to 50 years ago at a time that is considered by some to be a golden age. Figure 37 is the comparonomic graph that shows how much better off we are than 50 years ago.

The result of this analysis confirms dramatically how much better off we are than 50 years ago despite some economic models telling us we are not much better off at all. From an economic point of view, we are in 'the top 1%' of people that have ever lived — no one in history has ever had it better.

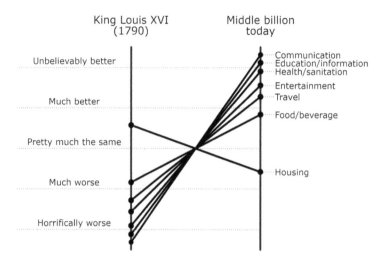

Figure 36 *Summary of how our life compares to King Louis's —*
most things are dramatically better. Source: Comparonomics.com.

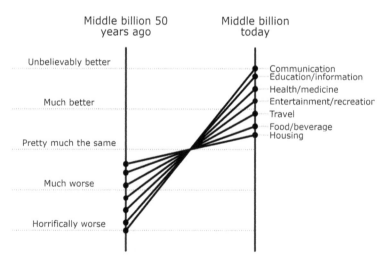

Figure 37 *Summary of how life compares to people 50 years ago —*
most things are much better. Source: Comparonomics.com.

Despite this clear result, the gloomy view of many conventional economic models that tell us we are no better off has made its way into public perception, and in my view it is brutally misleading.

To show that there is an alternative way to measure economic progress I defined a new term called speed of economic progress. This measures the speed at which goods and services make it from impossible to being available to everyone. Our rough analysis shows we have never been progressing faster (Figure 38). This is astonishing, wonderful news. New useful goods and services become next to free faster and faster (see Appendix 1).

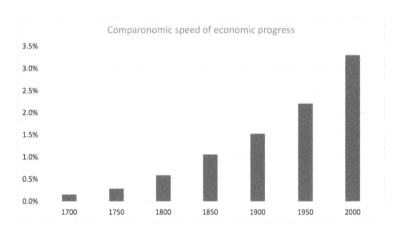

Figure 38 The speed of economic progress appears to be accelerating.

The last piece of analysis was to see how social trends have changed. Maybe these are the reasons that we feel so bad about progress. Figure 39 is the comparonomic graph showing social trends.

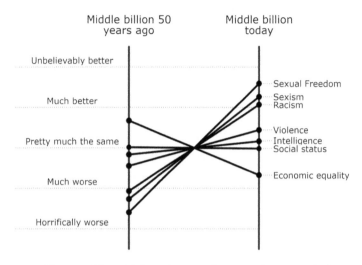

Figure 39 *Most social trends seem to be getting better over the last*
50 years. Source: *Comparonomics.com.*

The surprising thing about this analysis is that it shows we
have made significant strides in many of the social trends
that seem important to a lot people. Not everything has got
better, but on most measurable fronts we look to be vastly
better off.

SUMMARY OF PART TWO

How do we think we are doing?

A list of feel-bad factors that genuinely make us feel like things are not going so well has been defined. This has some similarities to the cognitive biases analysed in behavioural economics, but this list is specifically for long-term historical economic and social trends. The section below lists all the feel-bad factors and a brief description.

Summary of the different factors that make us feel bad about progress and life

Information-gathering biases

- *Media biased for bad news*: Bad news sells — we may have an evolutionary preference for bad news and media's aim is to sell, so that's what they give us.
- *Social media*: It is easier now to compare ourselves to other people but only through polished/edited versions of their lives, so we probably feel worse about our situation.
- *Pervasiveness of advertising*: Messages are shouted at us all the time, so we are encouraged to want more than we have.
- *Negativity bias*: Bad things are more memorable from our daily lives — accidents, arguments, so our memories are more likely to be full of negative things.
- *Digital screen addiction*: There is evidence that the

always-on nature of information from screens make us feel less satisfied.

Thinking biases

- *We now have time to think*: Hard problems of hunger, war, and plague are solved, so we have time to think about less significant issues — 'First World problems'.
- *Nostalgia bias*: The past appears better than it actually was. We believe our childhood and early years were idyllic.
- *Confirmation bias*: We continuously seek news to support current views, so it is hard to change how we perceive things.
- *Headwind/tailwind asymmetry*: Things that help us seem invisible (e.g. the tailwind of stable, safe democracy); things that restrict our progress are top of mind (e.g. the headwind of fake news).
- *Availability heuristic*: We remember stories about things we have recently heard more than data. This is not an inherently harmful thing but, when combined with bad news bias and confirmation bias, it exacerbates negativity.
- *Pessimism bias*: We tend to think bad things are more likely to happen. This is probably a result of the cumulative effect of the other feel-bad factors.

Social expectation biases

- *Natural level of grumpiness*: As a rule, grumping about things seems the norm and is expected to give stories of how hopeless things are no matter how much things progress.
- *Explaining how good life is seems unpopular*: Pointing out how great life is appears for some reason to be unpopular.
- *Cultural expectation of constant happiness*: People are expected to be happy all the time but this is not a realistic expectation, so we make an assumption it must have been better/easier in the past.
- *Need for social status*: Everyone aiming for high social status is a zero-sum game that not everyone can win.

Economic model biases

- *Economic models are wrong*: Having experts tell you how bad things are when in fact they not. The current models are not very good at the long-term analysis when goods and services change dramatically.
- *Nagging need for progress*: As a society, we feel the need to continually make economic progress. As soon as we have one thing, we are thinking about the next thing, which is always some time in the future.

Economic inequality biases

- *Inequality seems so unfair*: Other people seem to be doing way better – it doesn't seem fair in a lot of cases.
- *Some people can't participate in society*: Inequality means that some proportion can't join in with the rest of society. They don't have the resources to be part of what everyone else is doing.
- *Belief in meritocracy*: If you believe that your outcome in life is only related to your efforts, then you are likely to feel that any fault in doing badly is entirely yours.

I did not expect to come up with such a long list of factors that conspire to make us feel bad about progress, but it does explain the common perception of gloom despite the reality of comprehensive progress.

SUMMARY OF PART THREE

How can we do better?

Many of the standard things we aim for in society like economic growth, improved social mobility, and equality do not look to make an impact on most of the feel-bad factors. Even if we solved them all, we might not feel that much better — they don't get to the heart of why so many people feel dissatisfied.

There seem to be two promising ways of making us feel better about our privileged position in the historic 1%. The first is being aware of how good we have it and understanding that the feel-bad factors mean we will naturally feel worse about life and progress. The second, more controversial solution is to reject the idea of social status completely.

Table 4 shows the impact the proposed solutions have on the feel-bad factors. Dark grey indicates significant impact and light grey some impact.

Life is good by any objective measure compared to any time in history. A significant reason we don't feel that good is due to the zero-sum game of all striving for high social status. By opting out of the need for personal status, you can become free and make life more satisfying for you and those around you.

LIST OF FEEL-BAD FACTORS	Economic growth	Social mobility	More equality	Better models	Solving statusism
Media biased for bad news				■	
Social media			▦		■
Pervasiveness of advertising			▦	■	
Negativity bias				■	
Digital screen addiction				■	
We now have time to think				■	▦
Nostalgia bias				■	
Confirmation bias				■	
Headwind/tailwind asymmetry				■	
Availability heuristic				■	
Pessimism bias				■	
Natural level of grumpiness				■	
Explaining how good life is seems unpopular				■	
Cultural expectation of constant happiness				▦	
Need for social status					■
Economic models are wrong	▦			■	
Nagging need for progress	■				
Inequality seems so unfair		▦	■	■	
Some people can't participate in society			■		
Belief in meritocracy		▦			■

Table 4 Summary of how different solutions affect the feel-bad factors.

The nice thing about comparonomic analysis and policy conclusions is that you can get most of the benefits with no government intervention at all. No need to rely on the political process to come up with new legislation. You can choose to change your view on things, and life can end up significantly better.

FINAL THOUGHTS

The three parts of this book can be summarised in a super-short way as:

- Part One — We are doing great, so relax, enjoy, and be grateful (ignore those gloomy, old, inappropriate economic models).
- Part Two — There are a lot of reasons we don't think we are doing so well, so don't be so worried about the doom you may naturally hear about in daily life.
- Part Three — Understanding how well off we are may help free up some time to enjoy life or work on other pressing issues important to us. Being aware of these things and rejecting social status seems like a great way to live a better life for you and everyone else.

At the risk of sounding like a hippie, perhaps I could describe the book as a theoretical framework for why it pays to be nice to people, not to be envious of others, and to be grateful for all that we have. It's not that you haven't heard this before, but the evidence compiled here suggests that it will pay off both personally and for everyone else in the pursuit of a more meaningful, happy, and kind existence.

APPENDIX 1: ALTERNATIVE ECONOMIC GROWTH THEORY

Conventional economics is like a powerful, sophisticated electron microscope and comparonomics is a simple, cheap pair of binoculars. The body of this book shows how to use the simple new tool comparonomic graphs. I think it is useful in the form of graphs but in this appendix, I will expand on the binoculars a little bit to show how to build a mathematically precise tool. It is beyond the scope to fully build the more sophisticated tool but I will sketch some plans. Also, I have opted out of describing the sketch in terms that electron microscope users are familiar with (conventional economic jargon), as I want to make it possible for anyone to follow the core logic if they are not familiar with the terminology of economics.[1]

In Chapter 2 I created some mini thought experiments to conclusively show that we are vastly better off compared to even kings. It was also shown that we are much better off than folks from 50 years ago despite economic models suggesting that many people are no better off. The current way we measure economic growth does not include the fact everyone can have access to products that only the very richest could own a few years before. The comparonomic graphs showed this clearly in a diagram form, and this appendix explains how we describe them mathematically. I think the raw diagrams are more useful for most applications, but it could be boiled down to a new way of measuring progress that takes into consideration the speed at which new goods and services become available to everyone.

HOW CAN WE PUT NUMBERS AROUND COMPARONOMICS?

When comparing change between two time periods, the two simple questions I ask are:

- What is important to us?
- How have these important things changed over time?

I propose two new ways to measure these things that are different from conventional economics. Question one is normally taken as how much money do we spend on different sectors of the economy? Below I explain why it makes sense also to include how much time we spend on things from each economic sector, as this is also a strong measure of what we deem important.

How do we measure how things have changed when the types of goods and services change? Rather than critiquing how conventional economics does it, I am going to propose a new measure that looks at the time it takes for a level of good or service to go from being impossible to being available to the whole population.

WHAT IS IMPORTANT?

Time and dollars spent as an indicator of the relative importance of sectors of the economy

If we measure the economy, surely we only need to measure how we spend our money? What has time got to do with it? Once something is free, should it be included in any analysis of the economy? Let us do an absurd thought experiment. Imagine if productivity of everything — health, transport, housing, food — became so efficient that they were effectively free (like communications and digital photography is now). The only things we have not worked out how to make free are doughnuts and manicures. In this new economy, all economic output measures would be related to doughnuts and manicures. Everything else is free, so we ignore it — we measure our life history in some equivalent of constant doughnut-manicures. Kind of ridiculous but currently when things become free, they count for nothing because we don't spend money on them. While this example is silly, the mechanism is at work as economic history evolves. Most of the economy used to be agriculture — then as we mostly solved that it became a much smaller part of GDP. The same for manufacturing — it used to be a large chunk but productivity has increased dramatically and we spend less money on it. Overall, I would suggest these trends indicate great progress.

In some ways, time is potentially a more important indicator of what we deem important, as we all have the same amount of it and spend the same limited quantity every day (24 hours). How we allocate our time is the ultimate vote of what is important. If we spend time doing something, then it is probably more valuable to us than things we don't spend time on. Some things we spend little time on but lots of money, e.g. health (the ideal goal is to never go to the hospital but we still spend lots directly on insurance or via tax). Other things we spend little money on but vast quantities of time, e.g. TV, reading, internet, and hanging with friends and family.

I think it would be inappropriate to ignore money or time when asking the question of what sectors of the economy are most important to us. Exactly how you should combine them is arbitrary but surely it is better to combine them in some way rather than ignoring one or the other? We don't have to decide here how to combine them but point out that time should count for something. This is why during the book I included communication as a sector of the economy because if you break down how much you use this during the day, it is significant and hence important, even if it is next to free.

HOW HAVE THINGS CHANGED? HOW TO MEASURE THE SPEED OF PROGRESS

As the analysis in Chapter 2 shows, when the types of goods and services change dramatically, constant dollars are not a good way to understand how economies change. I propose a different measure. Let us assume that an economy is better if it is fast at making important things to us go from impossible to available to everyone. If it takes 50 years for a new thing we deem valuable to be available to everyone, that is slower progress than if it only takes 20 years. Remember, I am trying to come up with some way of measuring different things at different time periods. The rate at which the better things become available seems like a reasonable measure. We now have a numerical measure of the speed of progress where faster is better — we all get more things we value faster.

Definition of Speed of Economic Progress (SEP): 'The speed at which goods and services we find valuable make their way to the whole population.'

Let's define speed of economic progress as the number of years it takes for goods and services to go from the top 10% richest to 90% of the population. Yes, this is arbitrary, but then so is mostly ignoring these changes that people deem important. This definition is not the same as the time taken to go from impossible to everyone but it is easier to measure and will give the same relative speed of economic progress over time.

An alternative name for Speed of Economic Progress may have been Speed of Economic Diffusion, but that sounds a bit too technical, and I want to be sure that this is understood to be a way to measure how the whole economy is progressing. The Speed of Economic Progress (SEP) says nothing about the Gross Domestic Product (GDP), but SEP includes the idea that things in the economy can progress without the size of the GDP getting bigger.

Let's consider the example of Wikipedia taking over from the encyclopedia business. This caused a fall in GDP as the dollars spent plummeted from what was once a thriving sector of the economy. It probably also reduced the human suffering of forlorn salespeople drifting around door to door trying to offload tons of paper. As far as most people are concerned, we have a vastly better product (Wikipedia) with thousands of times more information for the cost of virtually nothing. The speed of economic progress shows this change as a good thing rather than a bad thing — speed of economic progress will increase. To say in some way that this change is bad for society because GDP and 'real' income fell is the whole point of this new model. Conventional economic models telling us life is no better can be brutally misleading.

Wikipedia is not an outlying example. Consider driverless electric cars. By some estimates, this could make travel vastly more accessible and safer but also cause a massive collapse in the old economy of making cars, mechanics, garages, and drivers. Bad for GDP, great for speed of economic progress.

Speed of economic progress can also capture parts of the economy not traditionally measured by GDP. Take an example of household work that if measured properly could be the largest sector of the economy.[2] Many devices have dramatically improved productivity here and by measuring the time spent and rate of adoption of new technologies, an estimation of speed of progress can be made.

I am far from the first person to point out that GDP is not a complete measurement of progress. Even Simon Kuznets,[3] who is the main inventor of GDP, pointed out lots of its limitations. Some of the other measurements that are useful include Human Development Index,[4] Index of Sustainable Economic Welfare,[5] Gross National Well-being,[6] and World Happiness Report.[7] Marilyn Waring's book *If Women Counted: A New Feminist Economics* is a particularly good discussion on the failings of GDP.

The speed of economic progress is specific in that all it measures is the relative speed at which things important to us go from impossible to available to everyone. I purposefully don't call it economic growth, as this has definitions that I don't want to mess with — but GDP does seem flawed by not properly counting things we find valuable.

AN ALTERNATIVE INDICATOR OF THE SPEED OF PROGRESS FOR AN ENTIRE ECONOMY

We can analyse an entire economy by splitting it into sectors and working out how important each part of the economy is (some combination of time and dollars). We can then look at the speed of progress of the goods and services in each sector of the economy. The example below is made up but shows that some sectors of the economy change faster than others and some sectors may be more important to us. Housing is slower than education/information, and health is somewhere in between.

We can also show the years taken for goods and services to go from richest to the whole population as a percentage. If it took 100 years, then it would be 1%, if it took 10 years then 10%, and 20 years 5%. Again this is an arbitrary definition but no less arbitrary than how we measure GDP. Table 5 shows how one could use numbers to describe an entire economy[8]. Don't worry so much about what the numbers are but, if there was an agreed way to calculate them, then this shows how they could be combined to work out a speed of economic progress for the entire economy.

SPEED OF ECONOMIC PROGRESS FACTORS	Relative importance	Years taken for economic progress	Percentage progress
Housing	27%	53	1.89%
Education/Information	24%	16	6.25%
Entertainment	17%	19	5.26%
Health	18%	23	4.35%
Transport	14%	34	2.94%
Average for economy	100%	30.28	3.30%

Table 5 Figures for an example economy where the relative importance and years taken for new goods and services to make it to the whole population can be used to calculate an overall speed of economic progress.

We could say that in this example the economy-wide speed of progress takes 30.3 years or 3.3% per year. This is obviously better than a slower economy where the change takes longer, e.g. 50 years (2%), but not as good as an economy with a speed of progress of 20 years (5%). Think of it as an alternative measure of economic growth that captures more things we deem important.

Imagine that we could create the same sort of analysis for any time in the past. I have not done this analysis but purely made up some numbers to reflect my guess that the speed at which the types of goods and services make it from the richest to everyone is increasing over time. I have not done this because I suspect other people would do a better job of it.[9] The numbers in Table 6 are a complete guess that includes one decimal place to create the illusion of precision that numbers have for some people (being explicit about this).

How you interpret these numbers is that in 1700 the poorest 10% of people had goods and services that people in the richest 10% people from the 11th century didn't have (623 years ago). Probably a more accurate number, in this case, is infinity, but let's go with 600 years. In the year 2000, the average speed of economic progress is guessed at about 30 years (as per the previous example). There are lots of things that everyone has now that no one had even 15 years ago (fast internet, smartphones,

YEAR	Years for progress	Percentage progress
1700	623.0	0.16%
1750	341.0	0.29%
1800	168.5	0.59%
1850	94.2	1.06%
1900	65.3	1.53%
1950	45.2	2.21%
2000	30.3	3.30%

Table 6 Estimate of the Speed of Economic Progress (SEP) over the last 300 years.

all sorts of medicines and entertainment options). In between 1700 and now I suspect the speed of economic progress has slowly increased. I guess that it will keep increasing.

When we graph this speed of economic progress, it shows that we have never been doing better and progress seems to be getting more rapid (Figure 40). I think this is a much more appropriate measure of the historical progress of our economy compared to the type of analysis that shows King Louis is richer than us despite living conditions that would be illegal for a prisoner today.

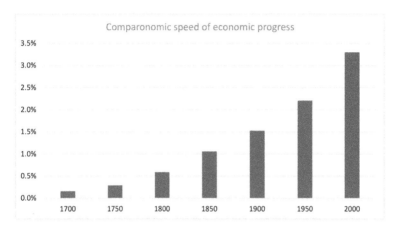

Figure 40 Speed of economic progress over the last 300 years.

It would be possible to update the speed of economic progress every year to measure how things are tracking, but it is inherently a measure that will not change that much in the short term.

The speed of economic progress is a new measurement tool that makes it easier to do a comparison when the types of things available change over time and when productivity increases so fast, those important things become next to free. I calculate this by an objective measure of how long it takes for things available to the very richest to become available to everyone. It also measures the importance of different parts of the economy based on both time and money spent. This definition is arbitrary, as is the current version that defines economic growth, GDP. It is not an easy task to make comparisons to things that are dramatically different over time. The current system of measuring GDP almost ignores many things (Wikipedia, Skype, GPS/maps, and digital photography) that are quite frankly amazing. Assuming free things are worth nothing seems like the worst sort of assumption, so hopefully, speed of economic progress is a useful additional measurement.

WHY IS THE NEW MEASUREMENT SPEED OF ECONOMIC PROGRESS (SEP) IMPORTANT?

I do not expect Speed of Economic Progress (SEP) to knock GDP off from being the main measurement of an economy. However, the new method of measuring how we are getting on solves significant problems with GDP.

- GDP measures things we spend money on but not time — SEP is a combination, hence a better indicator of what we deem important (as opposed to ignoring things when we have made them next to free).
- GDP struggles to account for the changes in types of goods and services. SEP measures the speed at which new goods and services make it to the whole population (as opposed to saying a phone is a phone despite the cost falling and features exploding).

Being told the economy is progressing faster than ever seems like a more accurate description of the reality of life given the comparonomic graphs developed in the book. I suspect if this was the message rather than the gloomy story told by inappropriate models, folks may have a more realistic and happy outlook on life and more effort spent on other problems we could be solving.

THE SPEED OF ECONOMIC PROGRESS IS NOT A MEASURE OF ALL ASPECTS OF LIFE

The Speed of Economic Progress (SEP) is not the ultimate measure of all aspects of life either. Life is a lot more than economic progress. Imagine if we solved health and old age magically. Ignoring the other implications of this, there could never be progress in health ever again, and this would not be a bad thing at all — health is solved. SEP would fall, but in this case, it would be great. The point of coming up with SEP was to illustrate how bad GDP is at measuring long-term economic progress. Conventional economic models telling us how hopelessly we are doing are brutally inappropriate and part of the cause of our gloomy outlook on life and possibly causing us to focus on the wrong problems.

What does the comparonomic view on life mean for how things will progress in the future? Google's chief economist, Hal Varian, came up with a simple rule, now called the Varian Rule:

> A simple way to forecast the future is to look at what rich people have today; middle-income people will have something equivalent in 10 years, and poor people will have it in an additional decade.[10]

I suspect we could refine this rule for different sectors of the economy that are likely to have different rates of economic progress. This could turn into a useful forecasting tool. Some sectors will take longer than 10 years and some shorter, and they may well accelerate at different rates as well. There are a lot of potentially exciting ways to play with this concept.

The question of what we should do given all this unprecedented progress is enough to fill another book. I love the analogy made by Yuval Noah Harari that the social and physiological tools we have evolved over thousands of years were designed to fight famine, war, and plague. Most of these things are solved. Now we are like firefighters without a fire. We are running around in full firefighting gear, mask, and axe flailing around on high alert. I suggest these firefighting tools are the feel-bad factors described in Part Two. These ways of looking at the world make sense if there are fires but not if you are on the beach on holiday. Perhaps we need to shed some of these biases that made sense in the past but now are suffocating and uncomfortable. Running around stressed on high alert may no longer be the appropriate default behaviour and may cause more problems than it solves.

APPENDIX 2: OTHER USES FOR COMPARONOMIC GRAPHS

THERE ARE many ways comparonomic graphs can be used for all sorts of problems. Within a day of giving the first draft of the book to someone they came back with a comparonomic graph that helped think about the new job they had compared to their old high-pressure corporate job (Figure 41). It not only makes it clear what part of the differences are important but also how important they are relative to each other. It is hard to think of a simpler way to show how someone thinks about the relative merits of two options.

It can also help understand people's completely different worldview with more sympathy. For example, I chose a few social trends that I suspect are important to many people (Figure 42).

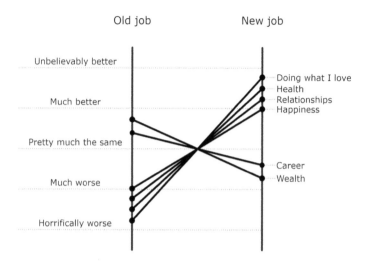

Old job   New job

Figure 41 Comparonomic graph comparing old and new jobs.
Source: *Comparonomics.com.*

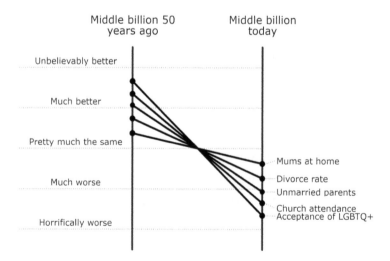

Figure 42 An alternative view of social change. Source:
Comparonomics.com.

However, if you are strongly religious, you could choose a completely different set of things that are important to you. Maybe the most important social trends to you are:

- Attendance at church/synagogue/mosque
- Divorce rate
- Children out of wedlock
- Acceptance of LGBTQ+
- Number of stay-at-home mums

Note that even then terms can be called different things depending on your beliefs. Rather than calling the change in what females are allowed to do sexism, in this version it is 'Mums at home'. This graph then becomes very clear why you may be upset with the changes in the world. It helps frame any discussion that you may have and I'd suggest allows more sympathy with different perspectives. More importantly it should remove a lot of talking past each other, as people can clearly see the things they deem important and how they see the change are completely different.

Comparonomic graphs could be used for a large range of other problems as well:

- The same analysis could be done for the last 20 or 10 years instead of 50 years.
- Apply the analysis to whole world, not just middle billion in rich countries.
- Analyse countries in a particular region or individual countries.

- Analyse groups within a country, e.g. youth, elderly, rich, poor, teachers, builders, and so on.
- Compare major event in your life, e.g. changing jobs, moving house, having kids.
- Change in your local environment over 50 years. Probably mostly better if you live in a rich country — less pollution, more protected areas, and more concern for the environment in community. It is easy to forget that 50 years ago, many rich countries were still destroying large quantities of natural habitat and this has now mostly reversed.
- Change in global environment over 50 years. Probably mostly worse — more population, more carbon dioxide, and less natural habitat. One of the things about realising how well we are doing economically is that it makes environmental and social justice causes seem more relatively important. Not tackling climate change risks seems like madness, particularly with the perspective that the economy is going better than ever ... Some estimate it could cost as little as 0.1% of GDP to stop the worst parts of environmental decline.[1]
- Direction of change in global environmental trends. Probably mostly better. Population growth slowing, carbon dioxide increases are slowing with clear path to dramatic reduction, and more habitat is going back to nature than being cut down.

There are limitless ways comparonomic graphs can be used to tease out any particular problem. You just need to ask two questions:

- What parts of the problem are important to you?
- How have these things changed?

Go to comparonomics.com and have a play or see how else other people are using the tool.

NOTES

WHAT IS THE PROBLEM?

1. Yes, I'm aware that reading old economics books puts me squarely in the economic geek zone but these thinkers have played an outsized role in how our world is shaped that makes them compelling. Schumpeter, Joseph. *Capitalism, Socialism and Democracy.* Routledge, 2013.
2. Keynes, John Maynard. *Economic Possibilities for Our Grandchildren.* Entropy Conservationists, 1991.
3. Kishtainy, Niall. *A Little History of Economics.* Yale University Press, 2017.
4. Kahneman, Daniel. *Thinking, Fast and Slow.* Farrar, Straus and Giroux, 2015.
5. Thaler, Richard H., and Cass R. Sunstein. *Nudge: Improving Decisions about Health, Wealth, and Happiness.* Yale University, 2008.
6. Term from book Evans, Alex. *The Myth Gap: What Happens When Evidence and Arguments Aren't Enough?* Eden Project Books, 2017.
7. Pinker, Steven. *The Better Angels of Our Nature: Why Violence Has Declined.* Penguin Books, 2012.
8. https://en.wikipedia.org/wiki/Availability_heuristic
9. Gardner, Dan. *Future Babble: Why Expert Predictions Fail and Why We Believe Them Anyway.* Virgin Books, 2011.
10. Gordon, Robert J. *The Rise and Fall of American Growth: The U.S. Standard of Living since the Civil War.* Princeton University Press, 2017.
11. Diamandis, Peter H. *Abundance: The Future Is Better than You Think.* Simon & Schuster, 2015.
12. Kurzweil, Ray. *The Singularity Is Near: When Humans Transcend Biology.* Duckworth, 2016.
13. Ridley, Matt. *The Rational Optimist: How Prosperity Evolves.* Harper Perennial, 2011. And Norberg, Johan. Progress: *Ten Reasons to Look Forward to the Future.* Oneworld Publications, 2017.
14. Pinker, Steven. *Enlightenment Now: The Case for Reason, Science, Humanism, and Progress.* Viking, an Imprint of Penguin Random House LLC, 2018.

15. Rosling, Hans, et al. *Factfulness: Ten Reasons We're Wrong about the World — and Why Things Are Better than You Think.* SCEPTRE, 2018.

16. Taleb, Nassim Nicholas. *The Black Swan: The Impact of the Highly Improbable.* Penguin Books, 2008.

17. Almost all of the criticism of Steven Pinker's book *Enlightenment Now* was about the analysis of why things change or how they might change in the future, which are inevitably debatable. I'm more interested in agreeing on how things had changed and working out why what we perceive is so different from reality.

18. The book *Factfulness* by Rosling, Hans, et al. has an excellent analysis of whole-world trends but the particular problem investigated in this book is about why us rich folks feel so grumpy.

19. http://www.oecd.org/about/membersandpartners/list-oecd-member-countries.htm

20. Rosling, Hans, et al. beautifully explains why focusing on the middle rather than the extremes can be a more insightful way to understand trends. They call it the gap instinct.

1. COMPARONOMIC GRAPHS: HOW TO REPRESENT CHANGE OVER TIME

1. https://en.wikipedia.org/wiki/George_E._P._Box

2. What the comparonomic graph does is allow you to engage in purposeful thinking. To make an accurate comparison moves from what Kahneman refers to as system one thinking to system two thinking. It transfers from a gut reaction to a more systematic analysis. Kahneman, Daniel. *Thinking, Fast and Slow.* Farrar, Straus and Giroux, 2015.

2. HOW DOES YOUR LIFE COMPARE TO KING LOUIS XVI'S?

1. Ridley, Matt. *The Rational Optimist: How Prosperity Evolves.* Harper Perennial, 2011.

2. Pinker, Steven. *Enlightenment Now: The Case for Reason, Science, Humanism, and Progress.* Viking, an Imprint of Penguin Random House LLC, 2018.

3. http://medicalhistory.blogspot.co.nz/2012/02/louis-penis-problem.html

4. Hanns-Peter Reisner, *Lektürehilfen Patrick Süskind, 'Das Parfum'*. Klett Lernen und Wissen, 2006.

5. Just pointing out that you can make these comparonomic graphs easily with a pen and paper.

6. Ridley, Matt. *The Rational Optimist: How Prosperity Evolves*. Harper Perennial, 2011.

7. http://www.dailymail.co.uk/news/article-3717348/Should-snap-cut-price-chateau-couple-did-swapped-two-bed-East-London-47-rooms-private-forest-moat-swap-pokey-flat-18th-century-castle.html

3. WHY COMPARONOMIC GRAPHS ARE IMPORTANT AND USEFUL

1. This number has been plucked out of the air, but precision sometimes falsely implies accuracy and believability.

4. HOW DOES OUR LIFE COMPARE TO 50 YEARS AGO?

1. https://www.commondreams.org/news/2016/12/22/historic-decision-canada-declares-internet-access-fundamental-right-all

2. https://www.theatlantic.com/business/archive/2013/02/how-airline-ticket-prices-fell-50-in-30-years-and-why-nobody-noticed/273506/

3. Hard to imagine but most cars didn't have them 50 years ago.

4. https://www.theatlantic.com/international/archive/2014/02/a-map-of-the-worlds-most-dangerous-countries-for-drivers/283886/

5. https://www.theguardian.com/world/datablog/2014/dec/29/aircraft-accident-rates-at-historic-low-despite-high-profile-plane-crashes

6. http://www.bradford-delong.com/2017/09/do-they-really-say-technological-progress-is-slowing-down.html

7. http://hortsci.ashspublications.org/content/44/1/15.full

8. Folks from the US may say they had air-conditioning 50 years ago. Yes, but we are talking about the average person in the middle billion, not just the US. All throughout these examples there will be bits that don't apply to you, but these are rough stories about most of the middle billion.

9. I'm not assuming all the middle billion have all these things but it's an example of things that would have been a lot less common in the past.

10. https://www.economist.com/united-states/2006/02/02/the-land-of-leisure

11. It is easy to forget how convenient things have become. After a day's travel and meetings recently, I just wanted to watch something mindless on TV in a hotel and I was astonished how unpleasant it was. You couldn't easily find something you wanted to watch. When the programme started, every 11–12 minutes the volume would go up and it would shout at you about stuff you didn't care about — the joys of advertising.

12. Tens of millions if you count something like YouTube.

13. Sim, Stuart. *Addicted to Profit: Reclaiming Our Lives from the Free Market*. Edinburgh University Press, 2012.

14. Taleb, Nassim Nicholas. *The Black Swan: The Impact of the Highly Improbable*. Penguin Books, 2008.

15. http://www.pewresearch.org/fact-tank/2014/10/09/for-most-workers-real-wages-have-barely-budged-for-decades/

16. https://www.statista.com/chart/23410/inequality-in-productivity-and-compensation/

17. http://www.pewresearch.org/fact-tank/2014/10/09/for-most-workers-real-wages-have-barely-budged-for-decades/

18. https://www.theatlantic.com/business/archive/2014/01/the-story-of-globalization-in-1-graph/283342/

19. https://www.telegraph.co.uk/culture/11349364/Why-we-yearn-for-the-good-old-days.html

20. Documentary film *Inside Job*.

21. http://prospect.org/article/40-year-slump

22. https://en.wikipedia.org/wiki/Declinism

23. http://www.pewglobal.org/2017/12/05/worldwide-people-divided-on-whether-life-today-is-better-than-in-the-past/

24. Gordon, Robert J. *The Rise and Fall of American Growth: The U.S. Standard of Living since the Civil War*. Princeton University Press, 2017.

25. https://web.stanford.edu/~chadj/IdeaPF.pdf

5. CHANGES IN SOCIAL TRENDS

1. Clearly not my opinion.
2. https://sciblogs.co.nz/mereconjecture/2017/01/07/1917-iq-intellectually-disabled/
3. https://en.wikipedia.org/wiki/Racism_in_France
4. https://www.theatlantic.com/sexes/archive/2012/12/more-women-are-doctors-and-lawyers-than-ever-but-progress-is-stalling/266115/
5. http://msmagazine.com/blog/2013/05/28/10-things-that-american-women-could-not-do-before-the-1970s/
6. https://en.wikipedia.org/wiki/List_of_elected_and_appointed_female_heads_of_state_and_government
7. https://en.wikipedia.org/wiki/Flynn_effect
8. https://www.oecd.org/els/soc/49499779.pdf
9. https://newrepublic.com/article/117558/can-income-inequality-be-good-society-conservatives-think-so
10. Piketty, Thomas. *Capital in the Twenty-First Century.* Translated by Arthur Goldhammer. London, 2014.
11. Stiglitz, Joseph E. *The Price of Inequality: How Today's Divided Society Endangers Our Future.* W.W. Norton, 2013.
12. https://en.wikipedia.org/wiki/Napalm
13. http://legaciesofwar.org/about-laos/secret-war-laos/
14. https://en.wikipedia.org/wiki/Zersetzung
15. I haven't found definitive evidence for this but it was a commonly told story to the tourists in Spain. Either way it is hard to believe a civilised democracy like Spain so recently had such a totalitarian violent leader as Franco. http://www.independent.co.uk/news/world/europe/spain-seeks-justice-for-final-victim-of-ailing-francos-garrotte-415202.html
16. Alan Turing, one of the greatest minds of the 20th century, was chemically castrated by the country he was instrumental in saving during the Second World War.
17. https://www.aclu.org/other/aclu-then-and-now
18. https://en.wikipedia.org/wiki/Interracial_marriage
19. http://news.gallup.com/poll/163697/approve-marriage-blacks-whites.aspx
20. https://en.wikipedia.org/wiki/Stolen_Generations
21. https://www.independent.co.uk/news/world/africa/when-french-police-turned-on-algerian-protesters-and-why-it-matters-after-paris-attacks-a6753716.html

22. https://en.wikipedia.org/wiki/Canadian_Indian_residential_school_system

6. IF THINGS ARE SO MUCH BETTER, WHY DO WE FEEL SO BAD?

1. https://www.economist.com/news/leaders/21712128-liberals-lost-most-arguments-year-they-should-not-feel-defeated-so-much
2. Harari, Yuval Noah. *Homo Deus: A Brief History of Tomorrow.* Harvill Secker, 2016.
3. Tversky, A., & Kahneman, D. (1982). Judgment under uncertainty: Heuristics and biases. In D. Kahneman, P. Slovic, & A. Tversky (Eds.), *Judgment under Uncertainty: Heuristics and Biases* (pp. 3-20). Cambridge: Cambridge University Press. doi:10.1017/CBO9780511809477.002
4. I say 'attempts' because I don't want in any way to equate the rough sketch presented here with the rigorous intellectual picture built up over the years by Kahneman, Tversky, and others.
5. https://en.wikipedia.org/wiki/List_of_cognitive_biases

7. INFORMATION-GATHERING BIASES

1. Kanouse, David E., and L. Reid Hanson. *Negativity in Evaluations.* General Learning Press, 1972.
2. https://en.wikipedia.org/wiki/Amygdala_hijack
3. https://www.economist.com/news/leaders/21578665-nearly-1-billion-people-have-been-taken-out-extreme-poverty-20-years-world-should-aim
4. https://www.theguardian.com/media/2015/nov/15/scientists-with-reasons-to-be-cheerful
5. Norberg, Johan. *Progress: Ten Reasons to Look Forward to the Future.* Oneworld Publications, 2017.
6. https://www.theguardian.com/media/2015/nov/10/week-off-facebook-denmark-likes-this-happiness-friends, https://www.happinessresearchinstitute.com/
7. https://hbr.org/2017/04/a-new-more-rigorous-study-confirms-the-more-you-use-facebook-the-worse-you-feel

8. Baumeister, Roy F., et al. 'Bad Is Stronger than Good.' *Review of General Psychology*, vol. 5, no. 4, 2001, pp. 323–370, doi:10.1037/1089-2680.5.4.323.

9. Steven Pinker, 'If everything is getting better, why are people so pessimistic?', Cato Policy Report, January/February 2015.https://www.cato.org/policy-report/januaryfebruary-2015/everything-getting-better-why-are-people-so-pessimistic

10. https://futurecrun.ch/

11. https://www.theatlantic.com/magazine/archive/2017/09/has-the-smartphone-destroyed-a-generation/534198/

12. https://www.sciencedaily.com/releases/2019/09/190930161918.htm

8. THINKING BIASES

1. Harari, Yuval Noah. *Homo Deus: A Brief History of Tomorrow*. Harvill Secker, 2016.

2. Franklin Pierce Adams.

3. Mortimer, Ian. *The Time Traveller's Guide to Medieval England: A Handbook for Visitors to the Fourteenth Century*. Simon & Schuster, 2011.

4. https://en.wikipedia.org/wiki/Rosy_retrospection

5. Mitchell, Terence R., et al. 'Temporal Adjustments in the Evaluation of Events: The "Rosy View."' *Journal of Experimental Social Psychology*, vol. 33, no. 4, 1997, pp. 421–448, doi:10.1006/jesp.1997.1333.

6. https://www.cato.org/policy-report/januaryfebruary-2015/everything-getting-better-why-are-people-so-pessimistic

7. All parts of the political spectrum can be caught up in this from the Greens harking back to the blissful life of hunter-gatherers or the worker parties that look joyfully when more people worked in steel mills and car factories.

8. http://freakonomics.com/podcast/why-is-my-life-so-hard/

9. https://www.economist.com/news/finance-and-economics/21723126-online-journal-encourages-economists-own-up-past-blunders-err-human

10. https://www.economist.com/news/books-and-arts/21729730-rarely-do-they-succeed-many-writers-try-span-americas-political-divide

11. Tversky, Amos, and Daniel Kahneman. 'Availability: A Heuristic for Judging Frequency and Probability.' *Cognitive Psychology*, vol. 5, no. 2,

1973, pp. 207–232, doi:10.1016/0010-0285(73)90033-9.

12. Just to note this doesn't mean we shouldn't have used stories in earlier chapters to show trends have changed. One story is not evidence but a set of stories about violence, for example, that are all much worse than now does build up a picture. And more importantly it is more 'available' to understand.

13. As quoted in Ridley, Matt. *The Rational Optimist: How Prosperity Evolves*. Harper Perennial, 2011.

14. I've spent a large part of my recent working life on an environmental project, as I can see a way to de-risk some of these issues. One thing that happens when we have a better understanding of how well off we are is that we are more likely to allocate time to other problems that need addressing.

15. Rosling, Hans, et al. *Factfulness: Ten Reasons We're Wrong about the World and Why Things Are Better than You Think*. SCEPTRE, 2018.

16. Gardner, Daniel. *The Science of Fear: How the Culture of Fear Manipulates Your Brain*. Plume, 2009.

9. SOCIAL EXPECTATION BIASES

1. As quoted in Norberg, Johan. *Progress: Ten Reasons to Look Forward to the Future*. Oneworld Publications, 2017.

2. http://www.datagraver.com/case/people-killed-by-terrorism-per-year-in-western-europe-1970-2015

3. http://psycnet.apa.org/record/2011-15463-001

4. https://www.economist.com/node/17722567

5. https://www.economist.com/news/christmas-specials/21732704-nationalism-not-fading-away-it-not-clear-where-it-heading-whither

10. ECONOMIC MODEL BIASES

1. http://www.businessinsider.com/millennials-uk-first-generation-1800s-do-worse-than-parents-resolution-foundation-2017-2?IR=T

2. http://www.pewresearch.org/fact-tank/2014/10/09/for-most-workers-real-wages-have-barely-budged-for-decades/

3. https://hbr.org/2017/10/why-wages-arent-growing-in-america

4. https://www.ft.com/content/e5246526-8c2c-11e7-a352-e46f43c5825d

5. Review in *The Economist* of *The Retreat of Western Liberalism* by Edward Luce.
6. https://www.psychologytoday.com/nz/blog/prefrontal-nudity/201603/expectations-dopamine-and-louis-ck
7. https://www.bbc.com/news/business-42538053
8. This argument does not hold true if you happen to have lost a job or home or something like that as a result of a recession. For most people, life still goes on much like before.

11. ECONOMIC INEQUALITY BIASES

1. Two Monkeys Were Paid Unequally: excerpt from Frans de Waal's TED Talk, https://www.youtube.com/watch?v=meiU6TxysCg
2. Harari, Yuval Noah. *Homo Deus: A Brief History of Tomorrow.* Harvill Secker, 2016.
3. Piketty, Thomas. *Capital in the Twenty-First Century.* Translated by Arthur Goldhammer. London, 2014.
4. de Botton, Alain. *Status Anxiety.* Penguin Books, 2014.
5. Michael J. Sandel's book *The Tyranny of Merit* is a compelling set of evidence on this topic.
6. Frank, Robert H. *Success and Luck: Good Fortune and the Myth of Meritocracy.* Princeton University Press, 2017.

12. SUMMARY AND DISCUSSION OF FEEL-BAD FACTORS

1. https://en.wikipedia.org/wiki/Optimism_bias
2. https://www.youtube.com/watch?v=VKHFZBUTA4k
3. https://www.cato.org/policy-report/januaryfebruary-2015/everything-getting-better-why-are-people-so-pessimistic
4. Nesse, Randolph M. *Good Reasons for Bad Feelings: Insights from the Frontier of Evolutionary Psychiatry.* Penguin Books, 2020.

NOTES

13. CONVENTIONAL GOALS TO MAKE LIFE BETTER

1. Easterlin, Richard A. 'Does Economic Growth Improve the Human Lot? Some Empirical Evidence.' *Nations and Households in Economic Growth*, 1974, pp. 89–125, doi:10.1016/b978-0-12-205050-3.50008-7.
2. Raj Chetty is one of the most articulate in this area of research: http://www.equality-of-opportunity.org/
3. Reeves, Richard V. *Dream Hoarders: How the American Upper Middle Class Is Leaving Everyone Else in the Dust, Why That Is a Problem, and What to Do about It.* Brookings Institution Press, 2017.
4. https://blogs.wsj.com/economics/2016/05/19/the-wealthy-in-florence-today-are-the-same-families-as-600-years-ago/
5. Reeves, Richard V. *Dream Hoarders: How the American Upper Middle Class Is Leaving Everyone Else in the Dust, Why That Is a Problem, and What to Do about It.* Brookings Institution Press, 2017.
6. Piketty, Thomas. *Capital in the Twenty-First Century.* Translated by Arthur Goldhammer. London, 2014. Stiglitz, Joseph E. *The Price of Inequality.* Lane, 2012.

14. MODEL MANIA — BETTER MODELS OF HOW THE WORLD WORKS

1. Unknown quote — but I like it ...
2. https://en.wikipedia.org/wiki/Stanford_marshmallow_experiment
3. Blackadder's insight shared with Baldrick.
4. I have a PhD in Ecological Economics, which is specifically looking at long-term issues of economic growth versus environmental damage.
5. https://blog.ted.com/what_are_you_op/

15. THE LAST GREAT 'ISM'

1. This has some similarities to the concept of rankism that is commonly defined as an assertion of superiority and putting other people down: https://www.huffingtonpost.com/robert-fuller/what-is-rankism-and-why-d_b_465940.html, https://en.m.wikipedia.org/wiki/Rankism.

The way I'd define statusism is broader than just the assertion of superiority but even if there is no assertion, there is a belief that people of high social status are somehow better than those with low social status. Maybe it's the same thing and maybe rankism is a better term. I also like the broadness of the term 'social status', as it feels like it covers more of life than just rank and it also links it closely to the economic concept of social mobility and social class.

There are other references to the idea of and term 'statusism' but I have not found any that define them in quite this way (e.g. credentialism from Michael J. Sandel). I haven't found a definitive first use of the term and don't want to claim to have invented it.

2. https://en.oxforddictionaries.com/definition/racism
3. I thought I was being funny with this one but apparently it is a thing. Apologies to all you hipsters out there.

16. STATUSISM — CHANGING HOW WE THINK ABOUT SOCIAL STATUS

1. https://www.brainyquote.com/quotes/j_k_rowling_178389 - also seems a bit odd that for a quote to sound right we have to say 'measure of a man...' not 'measure of a person...' Maybe one day...
2. https://www.economist.com/news/business/21719511-sales-bottled-water-overtook-those-soft-drinks-america-last-year-companies-are-racing
3. https://www.popsugar.com/food/Wine-World-Reels-2-Buck-Chuck-Wins-Award-404101
4. http://freakonomics.com/podcast/freakonomics-radio-do-more-expensive-wines-taste-better/
5. Gladwell, Malcolm. *Blink: The Power of Thinking without Thinking.* Penguin, 2006.
6. https://implicit.harvard.edu/implicit/
7. https://en.wikipedia.org/wiki/Robert_Solow
8. https://en.wikipedia.org/wiki/Paul_Romer
9. https://en.wikipedia.org/wiki/Behavioural_Insights_Team
10. Forgive the simplicity of condensing a superb 700-page work to two sentences — some nuances will inevitably be lost.
11. The policies suggestions are not as unlikely as I make them out to be, as there are certain places that are desirable irrespective of tax rates and it could be a general ratcheting to make this work. Still, it seems

incredibly unlikely given some countries are still lowering tax rates to be competitive.

12. Behavioural economics has taken a bit of the sting out of this where they have shown that you can get improved economic outcomes by changing your perceptions on thinking biases.

17. SUMMARY AND CONCLUSIONS

1. Kishtainy, Niall. *A Little History of Economics*. Yale University Press, 2017.
2. *The Economist* Christmas edition 2017.

APPENDIX 1: ALTERNATIVE ECONOMIC GROWTH THEORY

1. I know this is a little frustrating for academic economists but you can work it out. Also my apologies if I have not referenced all the appropriate literature I should — again happy to let someone else have all the fun of that.
2. Waring, Marilyn. *If Women Counted: A New Feminist Economics*. Harper & Row, 1988.
3. https://en.wikipedia.org/wiki/Simon_Kuznets
4. https://en.wikipedia.org/wiki/Human_Development_Index
5. https://en.wikipedia.org/wiki/Measure_of_Economic_Welfare
6. https://en.wikipedia.org/wiki/Gross_National_Well-being
7. https://en.wikipedia.org/wiki/World_Happiness_Report
8. There has already been much work done looking at the speed of technology diffusion, most notably that popularised by Clayton Christensen.
9. ... and maybe I'm lazy ... remember, I'm trying to do a really good broad sketch and let others more capable flesh out the detail and deservedly get the academic credit.
10. https://en.wikipedia.org/wiki/Varian_Rule

APPENDIX 2: OTHER USES FOR
COMPARONOMIC GRAPHS

1. https://www.theguardian.com/environment/2021/may/27/nature-financial-value-investing-global-gdp-avoid-breakdown-ecosystems-un-report-aoe

REFERENCES

Baumeister, Roy F., et al. 'Bad Is Stronger than Good.' *Review of General Psychology*, vol. 5, no. 4, 2001, pp. 323–370, doi:10.1037/1089-2680.5.4.323.

Bregman, Rutger. *Humankind*. Bloomsbury Publishing PLC, 2020.

Bregman, Rutger, and Rune Rogndokken Moen. *Utopia for Realists*. Spartacus, 2017.

de Botton, Alain. *Status Anxiety*. Penguin Books, 2014.

Diamandis, Peter H. *Abundance: The Future Is Better than You Think*. Simon & Schuster, 2015.

Easterlin, Richard A. 'Does Economic Growth Improve the Human Lot? Some Empirical Evidence.' *Nations and Households in Economic Growth*, 1974, pp. 89–125, doi:10.1016/b978-0-12-205050-3.50008-7.

Evans, Alex. *The Myth Gap: What Happens When Evidence and Arguments Aren't Enough?* Eden Project, 2017.

Frank, Robert H. *Success and Luck: Good Fortune and the Myth of Meritocracy.* Princeton University Press, 2017.

Gardner, Dan. *Future Babble: Why Expert Predictions Fail and Why We Believe Them Anyway.* Virgin Books, 2011.

Gardner, Daniel. *The Science of Fear: How the Culture of Fear Manipulates Your Brain.* Plume, 2009.

Gladwell, Malcolm. *Blink: The Power of Thinking without Thinking.* Penguin, 2006.

Gordon, Robert J. *The Rise and Fall of American Growth: The U.S. Standard of Living since the Civil War.* Princeton University Press, 2017.

Harari, Yuval Noah. *Homo Deus: A Brief History of Tomorrow.* Harvill Secker, 2016.

Harari, Yuval N., et al. *Sapiens: A Brief History of Mankind.* Vintage Books, 2015.

Harari, Yuval Noah., and Joandomenec (TRN) Ros. *Sapiens: De Animales a Dioses / A Brief History of Humankind.* Penguin Random House Group USA, 2016.

Harford, Tim. *The Undercover Economist.* Abacus, 2013.

Jalley Émile. *Thomas Piketty.* L'Harmattan, 2014.

Kahneman, Daniel. *Thinking, Fast and Slow.* Farrar, Straus and Giroux, 2015.

Kanouse, David E., and L. Reid Hanson. *Negativity in Evaluations.* General Learning Press, 1972.

Keynes, John Maynard. *Economic Possibilities for Our Grandchildren.* Entropy Conservationists, 1991.

Kishtainy, Niall. *A Little History of Economics.* Yale University Press, 2017.

Kurzweil, Ray. *The Singularity Is Near: When Humans Transcend Biology.* Duckworth, 2016.

Levitt, Steven D., and Stephen J. Dubner. *Freakonomics: A Rogue Economist Explores the Hidden Side of Everything.* William Morrow, 2009.

Levitt, Steven D., and Stephen J. Dubner. *Think Like a Freak: How to Think Smarter about Almost Everything.* Allen Lane, 2014.

Lewis, Michael. *The Undoing Project: A Friendship That Changed Our Minds.* Thorndike Press, a part of Gale, Cengage Learning, 2017.

Mitchell, Terence R., et al. 'Temporal Adjustments in the Evaluation of Events: The "Rosy View."' *Journal of Experimental Social Psychology,* vol. 33, no. 4, 1997, pp. 421–448, doi:10.1006/jesp.1997.1333.

Mortimer, Ian. *The Time Traveller's Guide to Medieval England: A Handbook for Visitors to the Fourteenth Century.* Simon & Schuster, 2011.

Mullainathan, Sendhil, and Eldar Sharif. *Scarcity: Why Having Too Little Means So Much.* Allen Lane, 2013.

Nesse, Randolph M. *Good Reasons for Bad Feelings: Insights from the Frontier of Evolutionary Psychiatry.* Penguin Books, 2020.

Norberg, Johan. *Progress: Ten Reasons to Look Forward to the Future.* Oneworld Publications, 2017.

Piketty, Thomas. *Capital in the Twenty-First Century.* Translated by Arthur Goldhammer. London, 2014.

Pinker, Steven. *Enlightenment Now: The Case for Reason, Science, Humanism, and Progress.* Viking, an Imprint of Penguin Random House LLC, 2018.

Pinker, Steven. *The Better Angels of Our Nature: Why Violence Has Declined.* Penguin Books, 2012.

Reeves, Richard V. *Dream Hoarders: How the American Upper Middle Class Is Leaving Everyone Else in the Dust, Why That Is a Problem, and What to Do About It.* Brookings Institution Press, 2017.

Ridley, Matt. *The Rational Optimist: How Prosperity Evolves.* Harper Perennial, 2011.

Rosling, Hans, et al. *Factfulness: Ten Reasons We're Wrong about the World — and Why Things Are Better than You Think.* SCEPTRE, 2018.

Sandel, Michael J. *The Tyranny of Merit: What's Become of the Common Good?* Penguin Books, 2021.

Sandel, Michael J. *What Money Can't Buy: The Moral Limits of Markets.* Penguin Books Ltd, 2013.

Schumpeter, Joseph. *Capitalism, Socialism and Democracy.* Routledge, 2013.

Sim, Stuart. *Addicted to Profit: Reclaiming Our Lives from the Free Market.* Edinburgh University Press, 2012.

Stevenson, Mark. *An Optimist's Tour of the Future: One Curious Man Sets out to Answer 'What's next?'.* Avery, 2012.

Stiglitz, Joseph E. *The Price of Inequality.* Lane, 2012.

Stiglitz, Joseph E. *The Price of Inequality: How Today's Divided Society Endangers Our Future.* W.W. Norton, 2013.

Süskind, Patrick. *Das Parfum.* Hanns-Peter Reisner. Kurt Lernen und Wissen, 2006

Taleb, Nassim Nicholas. *Antifragile Things That Gain from Disorder.* Penguin, 2013.

Taleb, Nassim Nicholas. *Skin in the Game: Hidden Asymmetries in Daily Life.* Allen Lane, 2018.

Taleb, Nassim Nicholas. *The Black Swan: The Impact of the Highly Improbable.* Penguin Books, 2008.

Tetlock, Philip E., and Dan Gardner. *Superforecasting the Art and Science of Prediction.* Random House, 2016.

Thaler, Richard H., and Cass R. Sunstein. *Nudge Improving Decisions about Health, Wealth, and Happiness.* Yale University Press, 2008.

Thaler, Richard H., and Cass R. Sunstein. *Nudge: Improving Decisions about Health, Wealth, and Happiness.* Penguin Books, 2009.

Tversky, Amos, and Daniel Kahneman. 'Availability: A Heuristic for Judging Frequency and Probability.' *Cognitive Psychology*, vol. 5, no. 2, 1973, pp. 207–232, doi:10.1016/0010-0285(73)90033-9.

Tversky, Amos, and Daniel Kahneman. 'Availability: A Heuristic for Judging Frequency and Probability.' *PsycEXTRA Dataset*, doi:10.1037/e301722005-001.

Tversky, Amos, and Daniel Kahneman. 'Judgment under Uncertainty: Heuristics and Biases.' *Judgment under Uncertainty*, pp. 3–20, doi:10.1017/cbo9780511809477.002.

Vollrath, Dietrich. *Fully Grown: Why a Stagnant Economy Is a Sign of Success.* University of Chicago Press, 2020.

Waring, Marilyn. *If Women Counted: A New Feminist Economics.* Harper & Row, 1988.

Wilkerson, Isabel. *Caste the Origins of Our Discontents.* Random House, 2020.

ACKNOWLEDGMENTS

The main people I'd like to say thanks to are all the nameless folks essential to any book getting published that seldom get mentioned. A hearty thanks to the folks who:

- work in bookstores
- print and distribute books
- take the time to write a review and share it
- teach our children (so we are sane for part of the week and can write and think)
- work in supermarkets and cafes to keep us sustained
- take our rubbish away, fix our roads and utilities
- and to all the other folks who do thankless tasks to keep society going.

I'm not trying to suck up to these people but they are all essential and I'd just like to acknowledge their usefulness. No book is possible without their roles so I'd like to say thank you.

The other key people that have made significant contributions but should take no blame for whatever faults are left in the book:

Gray Rathgen — key design help with the simplification of comparonomic graphs

Julian Cone — website wizard and all-round good guy

Clive Lind — superb editorial advice and encouragement

Sean Clements — magical skills for making it easy for anyone to make a digital comparonomic graph online

Martin Taylor — helped with the essential publishing details

All the folks listed in the references and footnotes whose ideas I have built upon. The three sources I used most often to guide me to interesting economic ideas were *The Economist*, Freakonomics podcast and London School of Economics podcast. Fantastic services to humanity — thanks.

People who gave valuable feedback on early copies of the book (too long a list to name).

Biggest thanks of all to my family for putting up with me while I worked on this.

And thanks to you for taking time to check out the book — it is appreciated.

Kia kaha

ABOUT THE AUTHOR

Grant is the son of an Invercargill chicken farmer who ended up a hopelessly addicted inventor. He has founded several technology companies in the area of internet search, social networking, personal electric transport and eco-tourism. For the past few years he has been working on a non-profit open-source project to protect New Zealand native species (cacophony.org.nz). He has worked as an advisor to the New Zealand Government in venture capital and science and technology policy. Grant has a degree in Mechanical Engineering and a PhD in Ecological Economics

comparonomics.com